Djekhy & Son

Djekhy & Son

Doing Business in Ancient Egypt

Koenraad Donker van Heel

The American University in Cairo Press
Cairo New York

First paperback edition published in 2012 by
The American University in Cairo Press
113 Sharia Kasr el Aini, Cairo, Egypt
420 Fifth Avenue, New York, NY 10018
www.aucpress.com

First paperback edition 2013

Dar el Kutub No. 7415/12
ISBN 978 977 416 569 6

Dar el Kutub Cataloging-in-Publication Data

Donker van Heel, Koenraad
    Djekhy & Son: Doing Business in Ancient Egypt / Koenraad Donker van Heel. —
Cairo: The American University in Cairo Press, 2012
    p. cm.
    ISBN 978 977 416 569 6
    1. Business—Egypt—Antiques   I. Title
    650.0932

1 2 3 4 5   15 14 13

Designed by Adam el-Sehemy
Printed in Egypt

Contents

Illustrations

Tables

Preface

This book was not primarily written for my colleagues, even though Egyptologists, demotists, and (legal) historians may think something of it and even use it to their advantage. The idea to rework my dissertation into a book for the general reader may be traced back to a question by a professor in Egyptology from Leuven, not long before his untimely death. He asked it some fifteen years ago, sporting a smile that has always stuck in my mind. In the course of time more people died and my wife and I became parents, an event that immediately answered any question one might have about the meaning of life. I also traded Egyptology for the communications business, so that my work (Egyptology) became my hobby and my hobby (writing) became my work. I now help people to sell things, but this never distracts me from those who are no longer with us. So goodbye August Eisenlohr, Eugène Revillout, Erick Schieferli Malix, Eugène Jansen, Jan Quaegebeur, Johan Govert Donker van Heel, and Wim 'Guitar' de Jonge. Let it be a comfort to you that 2,500 years ago there were Egyptians who would have turned your memory into a business case. This book is not about pyramids or Egyptian art and elevated religious concepts. This book is about ordinary businessmen from ancient Egypt.

The symbols used in the translations are as follows:

[. . .]   Papyrus is damaged or broken off
< . . . >   Omission by the Egyptian scribe
(. . .)   Translator's remark

Acknowledgments

This book has been in the making for some years, but it would never have appeared in print without the support of a great many people. Jean-Louis de Cenival, the late director of the Egyptian Department of the Louvre, gave me every opportunity to work on the original papyri of Djekhy & Son (and had me check all the loose demotic fragments while I was there), even temporarily assigning me to guard the Egyptian antiquities (and the telephone) in the *Réserve* of the Louvre while the staff went to lunch. His successor at the Louvre, Christiane Ziegler, has always been just as easygoing and supportive, being instrumental in the publication of some of the most difficult abnormal hieratic papyri the Louvre has to offer. Day-to-day assistance in the Louvre was given by Marie-France Aubert, Christophe Barbotin, Marc Etienne, Geneviève Pierrat, and Marie-Françoise de Rozières, all providing me with fond memories.

Maarten Raven of the Rijksmuseum van Oudheden (Leiden) granted his usual kind permission to make any use of the unpublished demotic P. Leiden I 375 (and no, I haven't forgotten that I promised to publish it). Permission to use some of the Turin ostraca recently published by Jesús López was secured through the courteous offices of Marilena Jerrobino, editor-in-chief of Cisalpino Istituto Editoriale Universitario (Milan). Nadine Cherpion and the Service des archives scientifiques of the Institut français d'archéologie orientale (Cairo) readily gave permission to use some of the documentary ostraca from Deir al-Medina published by Černý and part of Plate X from Vandier d'Abbadie, *Deux tombes ramessides à Gournet-Mourraï* (1954). Guillemette Andreu-Lanoë, the current director of the Egyptian Department of the Louvre, graciously authorized the use of the Louvre material. Zahi Hawass, secretary general of the Egyptian Supreme Council of Antiquities, very kindly allowed me to use some material from the *Catalogue Général*. Editor-in-chief Roland Enmarch happily permitted me to use a number of quotes from various issues of the *Journal of Egyptian Archaeology*. I greatly appreciate the kindness shown by all of you.

Sound advice on how to proceed with this book was obtained from Michel Chauveau of the École pratique des hautes études IV (Paris), Richard Parkinson of the British Museum (London)—who also gave permission to use some material from P. Phillips—and Janet Johnson of the Oriental Institute (Chicago). Ben Haring (Leiden University) and Huub Pragt (egyptologie.nl) helped out in other ways. Thanks are also due to the late Pieter Willem Pestman (Leiden University) and Sven Vleeming (Trier University), who came up with this subject many years ago. Thank you very much.

My former editor at the Economische Voorlichtings Dienst, Karin Hakkenberg van Gaasbeek, and Paulien Retèl critically read the Dutch manuscript, suggesting this English edition. Hans Schoens kindly prepared the maps of Egypt and ancient Thebes. The story of Djekhy & Son also owes much to the efforts of Randi Danforth and Neil Hewison at the American University in Cairo Press. They accepted my manuscript without hesitation and successfully saw it through to press. So now it is a book. Thanks!

My friend (and demotist) Cary Martin of University College (London) worked his way through an earlier version of the manuscript, uncovering some disconcerting errors and discreetly getting these out of the way. Any mistakes or oversights in this book are, of course, my responsibility.

Acknowledgments should end with those closest to one's heart. Constance, Lodewijk, and Emma: this is my book. I hope you like it!

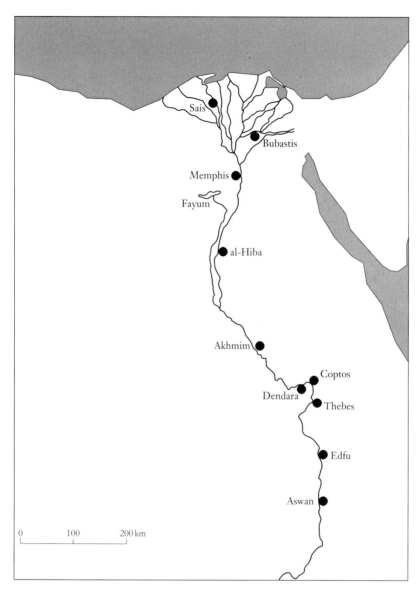

Figure 1. Ancient Egypt [Courtesy Hans Schoens]

Chronology

Twenty-fifth (Kushite) Dynasty
Shabaka   712–698
Shebitku   698–690
Taharqa   690–664
Tantamani   664–657

Twenty-sixth (Saite) Dynasty
Necho I   672–664
Psamtik I   664–610
Necho II   610–595
Psamtik II   595–589
Apries   589–570
Amasis   570–526
Psamtik III   526–525

Twenty-seventh (Persian) Dynasty
Cambyses   525–522
Darius I   521–486
Xerxes I   486–466
Artaxerxes I   465–424
Darius II   424–404

All regnal years are BCE. Note that all datings before the seventh century BCE are uncertain and also the subject of fierce ongoing debate. The dates used in this book were derived from J. Baines and J. Malek, *Atlas of Ancient Egypt*.

1

People

The Family

Djekhy son of Tesmontu was born in Thebes (Karnak) somewhere around 590 BCE, in the deep south of Egypt. His full name was Djedkhonsu-iufankh, which was a good Theban name. As happened so often with the ancient Egyptians, this was a theophoric name, meaning that it contained the name of a deity: 'Khonsu says that he will live.' But in daily life and official contracts he called himself Djekhy, just as Amunhotep was often shortened to Huy or Ipy, and—in the Dutch East Indies in the 1930s—my father Govert (Goofy) became Opy.

Egypt was not a stable country at this time. This period saw the definitive and forced withdrawal of the Nubian Twenty-fifth Dynasty that had controlled the south until then. In c. 592 BCE the Egyptian pharaoh Psamtik (Psammetichos) II took his army all the way from the north to the third cataract of the Nile, defeating the Nubians at Dongola. Psamtik's army took 4,200 prisoners of war, an event duly recorded for the benefit of the general public on a number of stelae, which served as an early government information or propaganda service. These stelae were mostly erected in or near the main temples for all to see. One of these, 2.55 meters in height and made of the famous Aswan granite, was found during construction activities near the old Aswan airport. It is now placed in the restored temple in New Kalabsha. It was engraved at a time when the dissemination of news was not immediate, but people had time to spare for public celebration. No doubt Djekhy's parents took the little boy out to see the victorious Egyptian troops return north, displaying their booty and Nubian prisoners of war, in ships sailing the Nile and marching on foot along the banks of the river. No doubt the great temple of Amun in Thebes did its share to celebrate Psamtik's victory with thanksgiving ceremonies, processions, and public banquets. When Djekhy's son Iturech was born c. 570 BCE, Egypt was racked by civil war between the Egyptian pharaoh Apries and his renegade general Amasis. In the end Amasis would be victorious, to become one of the most successful pharaohs in history. Iturech succeeded his father in the family business in c. 550 BCE. He had at least one brother, Khausenmin, who pops up occasionally in the family archive, as does a brother of Djekhy called Rery. In ancient Egypt families were much larger than today. It is very likely that Djekhy and Iturech more than once lost brothers, sisters, and their own children. Even the name that was given to Djekhy by his parents—'Khonsu says that he will live'—may be an implicit reference to the child mortality rate in Saite times. For this reason the family tree below is necessarily incomplete (the names of the women in the family are in italics):

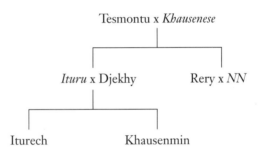

Tesmontu x *Khausenese*

Ituru x Djekhy   Rery x *NN*

Iturech   Khausenmin

Djekhy and his son Iturech were funerary priests who were paid to bring offerings to the dead. Today we would call them funerary service providers. Following the Greek rendering of their profession they are referred to as choachytes, water-pourers. For a remuneration of some sort they would bring offerings to the mummies in the Theban necropolis probably once a week, on festival days, on the birthdays of the deceased, and maybe even on the anniversaries of their deaths.

The actual working activities of the choachytes have been neatly summarized by the Dutch demotist[1] Sven Vleeming in his 1995 book *Hundred-gated Thebes* ("The Office of a Choachyte in the Theban Area"). The choachytes helped to prepare the funeral, took care of the—possibly temporary—storage and transport of the mummy, and if required also provided a final resting place that was either bought or leased. The

Theban choachytes of the second century BCE had a whole house built on the eastern bank of the Nile, to the west of the great Karnak Temple. Used as a depot for mummies waiting to be ferried over to the west bank, this house together with its garden measured 551 square meters. The very common tax of the overseer of the necropolis is probably connected with these mummy transports to the Theban necropolis on the west bank. The fee paid for a final resting place provided by the choachytes often also included such services as prayers and funerary offerings supplied by Djekhy & Son and their colleagues.

Djekhy and Iturech appear to have been prominent figures in the Theban choachytes' scene of the sixth century BCE. The personal and business archive of Djekhy & Son was found as part of a cache of documents related to the Theban choachytes, the earliest of which date as far back as 675 BCE, generations before Djekhy's time. Unless these papers belonged to Djekhy and Iturech's forefathers—something we cannot prove—we must assume that Djekhy & Son also kept documents for friends, family members, and colleagues; their forefathers may have done the same.

We can prove that Djekhy and Iturech acted as trustees for some of their colleagues. P. (Papyrus) Louvre E 7846, from 546 BCE, is a contract for a Mrs. Tsendjehuty that lays down the specific (and favorable) marital property arrangements she will enjoy in the event of divorce. She does not appear to have been related to Djekhy or Iturech, but other papyri show that members of her family, also choachytes, had close business ties with the family of Djekhy & Son. For an Egyptian woman in the sixth century BCE, this contract was the equivalent of an old age pension. In it, her husband had committed himself to maintaining her even if the marriage failed, for instance if another woman pleased him better. The only condition was that she not commit adultery, a circumstance described rather drily as "the large crime that is (usually) found in a woman." Quite a modern arrangement! The documentary sources from Egypt, some of which have been translated in this book, show that the ancient Egyptians were a highly practical people; Mrs. Tsendjehuty—however much she may have loved her husband—probably felt it safer to give this vital document to a trustee for safekeeping. This would explain how it came to be in the Djekhy & Son archive.

—᷍᷍—

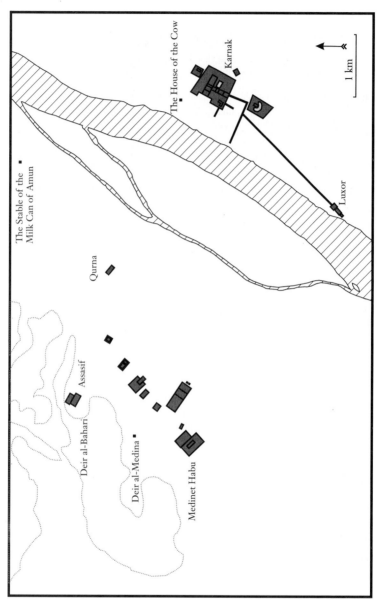

Figure 2. Ancient Thebes: East and west banks [Courtesy Hans Schoens]

Djekhy & Son acted as trustees because they were successful in their business. Among the mummies entrusted to their care was one belonging to the Besmut family, one of the most influential Theban patrician families in Late Period Egypt. Djekhy was granted land lease contracts to work the fields of the national elite, which could measure up to twenty-five hectares. His son Iturech himself owned more than ten hectares of grain (emmer wheat) fields located somewhere to the north of Qurna—obtained as a fee for his services as choachyte—which he leased out to other parties. In short, Djekhy & Son were doing very well by Egyptian standards. The papers from their archive offer clear insight into certain aspects of their lives, so for the first time we can actually rub shoulders with ancient Egyptian businessmen who lived, loved, worked, and died in Thebes some 2,500 years ago. This book is not about the ideal life portrayed on the walls of the ancient Egyptian tombs. Instead it takes us back to real life in and around Thebes, 550 BCE.

The choachytes of Thebes worked in the necropolis on the west bank of the Nile. This is also where most of their archives have been found, because the dark, dry tombs were perfect for storing important papers—better than their own homes. In a way, the tombs might be seen to have served as offices, where the choachytes not only worked but stored their equipment and files. There were, however, others in Thebes who could find their way in.

This is vividly illustrated by the famous case of a choachyte called Wesirweris, whose mummy store was pillaged by unknown thieves in 127–126 BCE. The thieves stripped the mummies of every valuable item, threw the bodies to the jackals, and walked off with all of Wesirweris's equipment, worth ten talents or sixty thousand bronze drachmae, according to his statement in the Greek P. Louvre N 2330. This would have sustained quite a large number of people for a year. In all, Wesirweris lost a few hundred kilos of bronze—an amount impossible to steal without some organization and planning.

Although they worked on the west bank, the choachytes actually lived on the east bank of the river in the densely populated quarters surrounding the great temples of Amun, Mut, and Khonsu in Karnak. In these times houses were generally small, and sewers as we know them didn't exist. It was warm throughout the year—very hot in summer—and city noise never stopped. It smelled. Getting sick in such an environment was not difficult; getting old was. It was always busy on the street and in the house. No wonder the Thebans sometimes grew irritated at relatively trifling things—if someone built an extension that blocked his neighbor's sunlight, for instance, or hacked out a window that looked straight into the kitchen next door. In the end, issues like these would have to be dealt with by the proper authorities, much as they are today.

In approximately 250 BCE an unknown Egyptian clerk wrote or copied a famous legal manual known as Papyrus Mattha (P. Mattha).[2] It is a collection of cases advising local judges how to proceed in everyday practice. The mere fact that a case was included in P. Mattha suggests it addressed an issue that had arisen more than once (P. Mattha VI 3–11):

> Suppose that someone files a complaint against someone else, saying: "Mr. So-and-So son of Mr. So-and-So has built a house on some undeveloped land, but the undeveloped land involved is my property, because it was the property of my father and he had a title deed made for me concerning it," and if the one against whom a complaint has been filed says: "It is my property, because it was the property of my father, and he had a title deed made for me concerning it," the judges will tell the person against whom a complaint has been filed: "Can you prove that the undeveloped land is your property, that it was the property of your father, and that he had a title deed made for you concerning it, or shall we leave it to the person who has filed a complaint against you to give proof that it is his property, that it was the property of his father, and that he had a title deed made for him concerning it?" Whatever the person against whom a complaint has been filed desires will be done.
>
> If he says: "I will furnish proof," and if he does not furnish proof, the house will be allocated to the person who filed a complaint against him and he must draw up a quitclaim for the person who filed a complaint against him.
>
> If the person against whom a complaint has been filed says to the judges: "Let the person who filed a complaint against me prove that this is his house," the judges will say to the person who filed the complaint: "If it is so that you have the honor, then prove that this is your house." If he then furnishes proof, they will allocate the house to him and his opponent will have to draw up a quitclaim for him.
>
> If the person (who lost the case) says: "Let it be permitted to me to take back the building material from the house," he will be allowed to take these away. If the person who filed the complaint

cannot furnish proof concerning the house, the house will be allocated to the person who built it, and they will order the person (who lost) to draw up a quitclaim.

The Egyptian authorities were quick to respond, effective, and compassionate and practical even in small issues. The case described below was apparently so common that even 450 years *after* P. Mattha was written it was included once again in a Greek translation of a legal manual from Oxyrhynchus very similar to P. Mattha (P. Mattha VIII 16–18 and P. Oxy. 3285, 32–37):

> Suppose that a person files a complaint against another, saying: "As far as the water drain of his house is concerned, it leaks water onto my house." The water drain will then be inspected visually and they will pour water into it. If the water reaches (the house of) the person who filed the complaint, they will cut off the water drain until it no longer leaks water on the house of the person who filed the complaint.

Let us return to Djekhy & Son. We do not know where exactly they lived in the busy quarters surrounding the great temples, but we can visualize one possibility, thanks to the research of the Belgian demotist Mark Depauw. In his book *The Archive of Teos and Thabis from Early Ptolemaic Thebes* (2000), Depauw investigated what had happened to a house that was owned by a certain Mrs. Thabis and her husband, the Theban choachyte Teos. This house was located in a quarter called The House of the Cow, a Theban neighborhood regularly mentioned in demotic papyri between 330 and 170 BCE. The House of the Cow was somewhere to the west of the large temenos wall of the temple of Montu and to the north of the great temple of Amun in present-day Karnak. Parts of this area were excavated by French archaeologists between 1945 and 1949, but their work mainly showed traces of massive burning at this spot at some time in the past. This is likely to have been the work of troops of the Persian king Cambyses, as reported for instance by Diodorus Siculus in *Bibliotheca Historica* I 46. It is certain that after this devastation no more building took place here, so The House of the Cow probably lies somewhat farther to the west. Both Amun, the Theban supreme deity, and the war god Montu were associated with a bull, and with this bull naturally came a female counterpart. The Greek name for this quarter,

Chrusopolis or Golden City, suggests that the cow involved was actually the goddess Hathor, who is once even referred to as The Mistress of the House of the Cow. If we assume that Djekhy's family lived in or somewhere near this quarter, their work at the tombs on the west bank of the Nile—in and around the Assasif—and on the fields in the agricultural area called The Stable of the Milk Can of Amun, located to the north of Qurna, would require a brisk three-mile walk at the very least.[3]

Depauw made a list of all the house owners in The House of the Cow, showing that in the Ptolemaic Period it harbored a mixed population of Greeks, high and low priests of the surrounding temples, a scribe of Pharaoh, a scribe of the district of Thebes, a teacher from the temple of Amun, all kinds of artisans including a coppersmith, several goldsmiths, a weaver of royal linen, and a stonemason, a baker of the temple of Amun, pastophoroi (bearers of the divine shrine), an eye surgeon, ritualists, and choachytes. Also exciting is that, according to Depauw's calculations, no less than a quarter of the houses in The House of the Cow were owned by women. By Egyptian standards the choachytes were probably well off, and one supposes that the same applies to Djekhy & Son, who lived several centuries earlier.

Neither Djekhy nor Iturech kept a diary, so we do not know what happened inside their homes. Apart from their names, the women in the archive remain unknown, as does Iturech's brother Khausenmin. His uncle Rery is mentioned in the official records of the Theban choachytes (P. Louvre E 7840), as well as in two papyri that do not belong to the archive and are now kept in the Egyptian Museum in Cairo as P. Cairo CG (Catalogue Général) 30657 and 30665. Both documents deal with a conflict, one a claim on Rery and the other his divorce.

Things become even more frustrating with regard to Iturech's personal life. We know that he bought himself a son called Hor in the spring of 539 BCE, but this is the only detail we have about the boy. Official records of the Theban choachytes written between 542 and 538 BCE mention various people who could have been sons of Iturech, among them a man named Anyuuchay, who was the chief financial officer or financial manager of the choachytes' association, and a choachyte called Khausenmin. If the latter is Iturech's son, he would have taken his name from his uncle. The final document deposited in the archive—P. Louvre E 7850, from 533 BCE—does not mention Iturech at all, even though he had been doing a great deal of business only the year before. Instead, this official letter is addressed to an otherwise unknown priest of Amun called Djekhy. Since in ancient Egypt people often named their children after their parents, it is at least theoretically possible that it is this Djekhy who is Iturech's son, named for his grandfather. But this would also mean that he had declined to join the family business Djekhy & Son, preferring a career in the omnipresent Theban Domain of Amun. Although not joining the choachytes' association would have carried the risk of social exclusion, this is a distinct possibility. Unfortunately, we simply have too little information to know rather than speculate.

Papyrus Mattha

P. Mattha—now kept in the Egyptian Museum in Cairo as P. Cairo JdE (Journal d'Entrée) 89127–89130 and 89137–89143—was found in Tuna al-Gebel, ancient Hermopolis, by the Egyptian archaeologist Sami Gabra during the 1938–39 archaeological season. The papyrus was named after the first man to work on it, the Egyptian scholar Girgis Mattha. P. Mattha is a legal manual dating to about 250 BCE, consisting of ten incomplete columns of up to thirty-two lines each in relatively easy Ptolemaic demotic. The cases described in this manual were designed to assist the judicial authorities by precisely describing how legal problems had been solved by Egyptian judges before them.

On the basis of internal evidence it was calculated that at least part of the original version of the text dates back to the eighth century BCE. We do know that parts of P. Mattha or a similar legal manual were translated into Greek 450 years *after* P. Mattha was written, in a document known as P. Oxy. 3285, after Oxyrhynchus, a location famous for the many papyri found there. This effectively means that by 200 CE there were people who no longer had a fluent command of demotic, but still needed to know and understand native Egyptian law. Recent finds suggest that many more versions or manuscripts of P. Mattha were circulating than just the one document now kept in Cairo. Probably each local temple or center of administration had its own manual. Girgis Mattha died without making serious progress towards the scientific publication of P. Mattha, which thus fell to the American demotist George Hughes (we will come to him again later) with his 1975 work, *The Demotic Legal Code of Hermopolis West*. This publication attempted to recognize Mattha's contribution by opening with his unfinished work and following that with a section written by

Hughes himself, which because of its completeness was vastly superior. The practical result, however, was that demotists had endlessly to leaf through this publication just to see who did what.

Many more of these legal case manuals have come to the surface in Egypt since 1975, often dealing with subjects totally different from those in P. Mattha. One of these papyri is P. Carlsberg 236, kept in Copenhagen. This papyrus is about the same age as P. Mattha and also badly damaged. Somewhere in the undamaged part, however, there is the heading '44,' meaning that in its original state P. Carlsberg 236 must have been at least 44 columns long, four and a half times as long as what remains of P. Mattha. The entire Carlsberg collection contains enough papyri to keep demotists busy for some time. According to the German demotist Friedhelm Hoffmann, thirty scholars could spend their entire lives analyzing and publishing the collection, and this is just a single collection from a small country.

2
Papyri

The Box of Muhammad Muhassib

In the winter of 1884–85, the German Egyptologist August Eisenlohr traveled through Egypt, one of the many Europeans who did so during that period. Eisenlohr—who should not be confused with his namesake, the politician August Eisenlohr (1833–1916)—was just over fifty years old. He could look back on a colorful career. He had begun by studying theology, but soon transferred to science and became a manufacturer of chemical products, a career he pursued for some years. And then one day—when he was already past thirty—he decided to become an Egyptologist.

Eisenlohr was not destined to become a great scholar, and it is no great loss that his *Ein mathematisches Handbuch der alten Ägypter* (1877) has fallen out of fashion. Yet by 1872 he had managed to become an extraordinary professor of Egyptology in Heidelberg. And by 1884, here he was in Egypt, trying to beat off not just the countless flies, but also many agitated local dealers in Egyptian antiquities. Even a quiet breakfast in the hypostyle hall of the Karnak Temple was out of the question, because each morning dealers crowded around his table, hoping to sell him something.

One day, however, he was approached by the antiquities dealer Muhammad Muhassib. Muhassib (1843–1928) was a bona fide dealer in antiquities. He had a good reputation. He was, for instance, one of the dealers favored by E.A. Wallis Budge of the British Museum. There is probably not a single official collection of Egyptian antiquities in the world that does not include a piece handled by Muhassib. He started out as a donkey boy, but one day attracted the attention of the famous fashion designer Lady Lucie Duff Gordon. In her days Duff Gordon was a true celebrity. It was from her that Muhassib learned the basics of the English language.

Muhassib carried a large tin box that was filled to the brim with rolled-up ancient Egyptian papyri. Nobody will ever know exactly how much Eisenlohr paid Muhassib to acquire them. It was a quick purchase, no questions asked, and Eisenlohr took the papyri to his boat on the Nile. There he unrolled them together with the Austrian Egyptologist Jakob Krall—a job Egyptologists nowadays leave to specialists. Jakob Krall was in Egypt to buy antiquities for the Kunsthistorisches Museum in Vienna. He had been partly trained at the Collège de France in Paris and he could also read demotic, an extremely abbreviated rendering of the hieroglyphic script that began to replace hieratic as the everyday script in the seventh century BCE. From an Egyptological point of view, Eisenlohr hit the jackpot on that day.

In a letter to a friend, Eisenlohr described what he had bought from Muhassib: a large number of ancient Egyptian legal contracts dating back to a period between the twelfth and thirty-seventh regnal years of Pharaoh Amasis, who ruled from 570 to 526 BCE; a contract from the reign of Apries (589–570 BCE)—the biblical Hophra; and a number of contracts from the reign of one or more pharaohs called Psamtik. In Eisenlohr's days Egyptologists only vaguely suspected that in this period—referred to as the Saite Period after the capital Sais (modern Sa al-Hajar) in the Delta—the Egyptians used two different scripts. Hieroglyphs were actually only used on the walls of temples and tombs or for other monumental inscriptions like stelae. In daily life, however, the Egyptians in the Delta wrote in a shorthand script developed from hieratic. This is called early demotic. A second shorthand script—developed more or less simultaneously in the Theban region in the deep south of Egypt—is called abnormal hieratic. Nobody could read this in the nineteenth century. Even today most Egyptologists are obliged to rely on the handful of people who can. Still, in his letter Eisenlohr wrote about the contracts he had bought that the metal box contained a number of papyri that strongly reminded him of the abnormal hieratic contracts he had seen in the Museo Egizio in Turin. Even if Eisenlohr couldn't read the script, his memory and perceptiveness were acute.

Eisenlohr's luck held. On the way home to Heidelberg, a thief broke into his cabin and made off with some bronze artifacts—he may have mistaken them for gold—leaving the papyri unharmed. Indeed, it was our luck as much as Eisenlohr's; who knows where this collection would have ended up had it been stolen that night? In the late nineteenth-century antiquities trade it often happened that a perfectly preserved papyrus would be cut in half to double its market price. A famous example is P. Amherst-Leopold, a text dealing with the royal tomb robberies in the reign of Ramesses IX (ruled 1131–1112 BCE). The lower half was bought in Egypt in the nineteenth century by Lord Amherst of Hackney, who sold it to John Pierpont Morgan in 1913. The upper half was found by the Belgian Egyptologist Jean Capart in 1935, hidden in a small wooden statue kept at the Musées royaux d'Art et d'Histoire in Brussels. He named it P. Leopold II after the Belgian king who supposedly bought this statue in Egypt, in either 1854 or 1862. As we said, this was Eisenlohr's lucky day.

Perhaps at the bidding of Jakob Krall, who had some connections to the Louvre, Eisenlohr wrote a letter to the conservator of the Egyptian department, Eugène Revillout, to tell him about the purchase. It seems Revillout appeared at his doorstep in Heidelberg more or less within days.

In Egyptology—or, to be more precise, in demotic studies that deal with the native script and culture from the Saite up to and including the Roman Period—Revillout occupies a special place. He was one of the true pioneers in the decipherment of demotic and the documents written in this script, often legal contracts that teach us more about ancient Egypt than perhaps slightly overrated sources such as the Book of the Dead or the mask of Tutankhamun. These contracts deal mostly with the sale of houses and other items, land leases, and marital property settlements, but there are also inventories, letters, process protocols, and a very rich literature. Revillout visited and studied all the important Egyptian collections in Europe and wrote impressively big books about them that were sometimes published as facsimile editions. In spite of his brilliance—or perhaps because of it—Revillout was not a very nice man, and by the end of his career he had started to turn sour when the torch was taken over by a whole new generation of Egyptologists better able to deal effectively with early demotic and abnormal hieratic, men like Wilhelm Spiegelberg and Georg Möller in Germany and Francis Llewellyn Griffith in England. It must have been gruesome to Revillout that—even though this new generation of Egyptologists always faithfully referred to the work done by him—their own work was not only scientifically verifiable, but also far superior to his own. A hundred years later many of these second-generation publications are still very useful, whereas Revillout's work has become obsolete with time. One would, for instance, very much like to know whether Revillout ever saw Griffith's masterpiece (almost unsurpassed to this day), the first edition of the early demotic Rylands papyri from Manchester in 1909 (see "Papyrus Rylands 9" in chapter 5), understanding that his days were over. He died soon afterwards in 1913. But this wasn't the end. Many years later, one day none other than Michel Malinine, the Russian-French demotist who was the first to publish a large number of the papyri from the Eisenlohr collection (which is the subject of this book), was walking the streets of Paris when suddenly he saw a photograph of an early demotic papyrus sticking out of a dustbin. Of course he went to look. It turned out that the descendants of Revillout had been busy for some days cleaning away the papers of the late professor Eugène Revillout. *Sic transit gloria mundi.*

But in 1885 Revillout was still on top of things. On that beautiful day, as he sat in Eisenlohr's study in Heidelberg, looking at a stunning collection of ancient Egyptian papyri, his knowledge of demotic allowed him to recognize immediately that this collection was unique. He wasted no time; on 18 June 1885 the papyri were sold to him in a notary office in Heidelberg, for a significant price. The Louvre agreed to pay 25,000 old French francs, the equivalent of about €100,000 today. Joint publication of the papyri followed soon thereafter, probably as part of the deal of sale. Between 1885 and 1902 Revillout and Eisenlohr published their *Corpus Papyrorum Aegypti*, containing the photographs of twelve papyri, accompanied by Revillout's now obsolete translations. The photos—or *héliogravures*, as they were called—are still exquisite, but are not entirely reliable, as will be seen later.

What was so special about this collection sold by Eisenlohr? According to Revillout's own description of the sale, there were thirty-one papyri, one from the Ptolemaic Period and thirty from the Late Period. At present, these papyri are known as numbers E 7832–7862 of the Louvre's *Livre d'inventaire*. The early demotic papyri that Revillout could read (up to a point) were the first he entered in the museum's inventory. Those written in abnormal hieratic, however, were virtually incomprehensible to him and so were entered later (which makes sense; to give a good description of a papyrus you must know what it says). The fact that some of these papyri have only recently been published because no one had been able to read them sheds light on the difficulty and frustration Revillout must

Table 1. Basic inventory of the Djekhy & Son archive

No.	Year BCE	Script	Subject
7832	539	Early demotic	Purchase of a son
7833	535	Early demotic	Land lease
7834	536	Early demotic	Receipt for harvest tax
7835	537	Early demotic	Receipt for harvest tax
7836	536	Early demotic	Land lease
7837	535	Early demotic	Land lease
7838	536	Early demotic	Receipt for harvest tax
7839	534	Early demotic	Land lease
7840	542–538	Early demotic	Records of choachytes' association
7841	559	Early demotic	Receipt for harvest tax
7842	540	Early demotic	Receipt for harvest tax
7843	536	Early demotic	Business partnership
7844	555	Early demotic	Land lease
7845	554	Early demotic	Land lease
7846	546	Abnormal hieratic	Marital property settlement
7847	552	Abnormal hieratic	Receipt
7848	558	Abnormal hieratic	Hostile takeover of a tomb
7849	590	Abnormal hieratic	Marital property settlement
7850	533	Early demotic	Official letter
7851	665	Abnormal hieratic	Land lease
7852	c. 675	Abnormal hieratic	Land lease
7853	572	Abnormal hieratic	Legal conflict?
7854	after 550	Early demotic	Official letter
7855	559	Early demotic	Letter
7856	672	Abnormal hieratic	Land lease
7857	590	Abnormal hieratic	—
7858	609	Abnormal hieratic	Donation of land
7859	578	Abnormal hieratic	—
7860	584	Abnormal hieratic	Land lease
7861	568	Abnormal hieratic	Business conflict
7862	118	Ptolemaic demotic	Division of a house

have felt. On the other hand, in his day and age nobody could check his entries in the *Livre d'Inventaire* either, so in the case of most of the abnormal hieratic items he more or less made things up as he went along.

We do not know whether Revillout told Eisenlohr, on this day in Heidelberg, just what made his collection so unique: many of the papyri came from the personal archive of two Egyptian businessmen from the sixth century BCE, a man called Djekhy and his son Iturech, from the firm Djekhy & Son. With these papyri, Egyptologists were suddenly offered a glimpse into the lives of two rather ordinary Egyptians from the Saite Period—not as they would have portrayed themselves on the walls of their tombs, but through the details contained in legal contracts drawn up by Egyptian scribes in Thebes some 2,500 years ago. They also collected their own archive as Djekhy & Son.

The Archive of Djekhy & Son

Today, the archive of Djekhy & Son is kept in the Louvre in Paris under the inventory numbers P. Louvre E 7832–7862 (see Table 1).

However, things usually go wrong if people are involved. People forget about the correct inventory numbers, mix them up, use them twice, or simply read them the wrong way. As a result, following Revillout's purchase of the Eisenlohr collection and owing to the efforts of Egyptologists from all over the world, the papyri can also be listed as Table 2 shows.

Some of these ghost numbers can be traced back directly to Revillout. Apparently his compositor—in those days book pages were still hand-set using letters made of cast lead—was not always able to distinguish between Revillout's handwritten 1 and 7, and if Revillout read the proofs, he did not notice this mistake. A single small mistake could thus produce up to six ghost numbers, and the confusion to match. One of the ghost papyri seemed especially interesting. In his *Notice des papyrus démotiques archaïques et autres textes juridiques ou historiques* (1896), Revillout mentioned a Papyrus de Londres no. 50, kept in the British Museum, which was about the choachyte Djekhy, son of Tesmontu and the first known owner of the Djekhy & Son archive. It so happens that the Egyptian collection of the British Museum contains at least two papyri mentioning Djekhy: P. BM EA (Egyptian Antiquities) 10113 and 10432. Revillout's notes suggested that there might be a third, but it was a false trail. His Papyrus de Londres no. 50 is probably P. BM EA 10382/6, a papyrus that has nothing to do with Djekhy at all. This was not, however, the only promising lead. During the Polish excavations at Deir al-Bahari in April 1964, the team found a number of small fragments of a hieratic papyrus of eleven by seventeen centimeters that yielded eighteen lines of Chapter 146 of the Book of the Dead. It received the inventory number F. 5594, was deposited in an Egyptian storehouse containing the Polish finds from the temple of Thutmosis III, and was never heard from again. The excavators dated the papyrus somewhere between the Saite and the Ptolemaic periods. This Book of the Dead was written for a man called "the Osiris (i.e., deceased) Iturech true of voice son of likewise (Osiris) Djekhy [true of voice],"—the square brackets indicating a lacuna. This would have been a sensational find if the story had ended here, but it goes on. The same excavators found parts of a sarcophagus belonging to an overseer of the priests of Min Lord of Panopolis, who was also an overseer of the priests of Horus Lord of Aphroditopolis, as well as of the priests of Wepwawet Lord of Asyut. His name was Iturech and his father was a priest of Montu called Djekhy. This path too, however, proved a dead end. A previous publication by the French Egyptologist Henri Gauthier of the original text from the bottom of the sarcophagus had revealed that the mother of this Iturech was called Tsenese, and so these were not the same men as those behind Djekhy & Son.

P. Louvre E 7834 and 7838

Archival research is fraught with promising but ultimately disappointing leads, but it sometimes also brings to light unknown facts. Take, for instance, the muddle around P. Louvre E 7834 and 7838. These two papyri are so similar that until 1996, the scientific literature referred to each one wrongly as the other. It is not difficult to see why: they were written by the same scribe on the same day, they are both receipts for harvest tax, and both mention the choachyte Iturech, the second known owner of the archive. Both receipts were signed by the same witnesses in the same order. In P. Louvre E 7838 Iturech acts on his own, whereas in P. Louvre E 7834 he is accompanied by two business partners. The mix-up may date as far back as Revillout himself, but for decades no one looked carefully enough at the original papyri in the Louvre to see the mistake. When it was discovered in 1992, the then head of the Egyptian department, Jean-Louis de Cenival, simply said to the Dutch demotist who came running to report his discovery, in a manner that was both elegant and very French: "Well, in that case let's just switch the inventory numbers, shall we?"

Table 2. Revised inventory of the Djekhy & Son archive

No.	Year BCE	Script	Subject
1833			= 7833 and 7837
1834			= 7834 and 7838
1836			= 7836
1838			= 7838 and 7834
1840*bis*			= 7840
1843			= 7843
1861			= 7861
7340			= 7840
7450			= 7850
7832	539	Early demotic	Purchase of a son
7833	535	Early demotic	Land lease
7833A			= 7833
7833B			= 7837
7834	536	Early demotic	Receipt for harvest tax = 7834 and 7838
7835	537	Early demotic	Receipt for harvest tax
7836	536	Early demotic	Land lease
7837	535	Early demotic	Land lease
7838	536	Early demotic	Receipt for harvest tax = 7838 and 7834
7839	534	Early demotic	Land lease
7840	542–538	Early demotic	Records of choachytes' association
7840*bis*			= 7840
7841	559	Early demotic	Receipt for harvest tax
7841*bis*			= 7840
7842	540	Early demotic	Receipt for harvest tax
7843	536	Early demotic	Business partnership
7844	555	Early demotic	Land lease
7845			= 7845A
7845A	554	Early demotic	Land lease
7845B	after 554	Abnormal hieratic	Division of harvest
7845C		Abnormal hieratic	Belongs to 7858

No.	Year BCE	Script	Subject
7846	546	Abnormal hieratic	Marital property settlement
7847	552	Abnormal hieratic	Receipt
7847A			= 7847
7848	558	Abnormal hieratic	Hostile takeover of a tomb
7849	590	Abnormal hieratic	Marital property settlement (+ 7857A + 7857B)
7850	533	Early demotic	Official letter
7851*ro*	665	Abnormal hieratic	Land lease
7851*vo*	665	Abnormal hieratic	Land lease
7852	c. 675	Abnormal hieratic	Land lease
7853	572	Abnormal hieratic	Legal conflict?
7854	after 550	Early demotic	Official letter
7855	559	Early demotic	Letter
7856*ro*	672	Abnormal hieratic	Land lease
7856*vo*	672	Abnormal hieratic	Land lease
7856C	—	Abnormal hieratic	—
7857A	590	Abnormal hieratic	Belongs to 7849
7857B	590	Abnormal hieratic	Belongs to 7849
7857C	609	Abnormal hieratic	Belongs to 7858
7858	609	Abnormal hieratic	Donation of land (+ 7845C + 7857C)
7859*ro*	578	Abnormal hieratic	—
7859*vo*	—	Abnormal hieratic	—
7860	584	Abnormal hieratic	Land lease
7861	568	Abnormal hieratic	Business conflict
7862	118	Ptolemaic demotic	Division of a house

ro = recto (front), *vo* = verso (back) of a papyrus

One of the scholars who has always been very keen on making early demotic—and any demotic for that matter—accessible to students was the Danish demotist Wolja Erichsen. It was he who published the still indispensable *Demotisches Glossar* (1954), which has remained the only useful demotic dictionary for the past fifty years.[1] He was also the artist behind a dictionary that was to become the ultimate monument for the ancient Egyptian language, the *Wörterbuch der Ägyptischen Sprache*, a venture undertaken by the German Egyptologists Adolf Erman, Kurt Sethe, and Hermann Grapow in 1897. Supported by colleagues from all over the world, they collected, studied, stored, and processed all the words then known on all extant ancient Egyptian remains, from stela to tomb wall. In total, the dictionary comprised one and a half million fiches. Parts I to V—all drawn and handwritten by Erichsen—were published between 1926 and 1931, to be followed by a number of volumes containing the references.

One of Erichsen's publications that is still used to acquaint students with demotic is his *Auswahl frühdemotischer Texte zum Gebrauch im akademischen Unterricht sowie zum Selbststudium zusammengestellt* (1950), which also contains facsimiles of P. Louvre E 7834 and 7838. As with many other scientific publications on these texts, the *Auswahl* had listed these papyri under the wrong (opposite) inventory numbers. The brilliance of de Cenival's elegant solution is that with one simple change, all references not just in the *Auswahl*, but indeed all other scientific publications mentioning these receipts, are correct once again.

In P. Louvre E 7834, Iturech was accompanied by two business partners who appear often in the archive of Djekhy & Son. They came to pay their sizable harvest tax, about thirty-seven sacks of emmer, each one—divided into four oipe—being about eighty liters:

Regnal year 35, first month of the peret season under Pharaoh l.p.h. Amasis l.p.h.[2] Entered as received from the cattle keeper of the Domain of Montu Ituru son of Pawakhamun, and ditto (i.e., of the same profession) his brother Petemontu and the choachyte Iturech son of Djekhy, together three men, delivered into the hand of the scribes of the Domain of Amun in the district of Coptos: the harvest tax of the Domain of Amun for the fields that they tilled in the west from regnal year 34 to regnal year 35. Emmer 37 (sacks and) 1/6 (oipe, measured with) the oipe of 40 hin, in full. I have received them. Their hearts are satisfied with them, they being complete, without remainder. In the handwriting of Petemestu son of Horsiese, the scribe of the mat.

In the handwriting of Khonsuirtais son of Djedmutiufankh.

In the handwriting of Djedkonsuiufankh son of Rery.

In the handwriting of Petehorresne son of Khedebkhonsuirbin.

In the handwriting of Horwedja son of Wennefer, the scribe of the Domain of Amun in the district of Coptos.

In the handwriting of Petosiris son of Khedebkhonsuirbin.

In the handwriting of Neswennefer son of Sobekemhat regarding his emmer, 37 (sacks and) 1/6 (oipe, measured with) the oipe of 40 hin, in full and abovementioned.

The Louvre papyri that form part of the Eisenlohr collection can be dated from about 675 to 118 BCE. It is unknown how the Egyptian antiquities dealer Muhammad Muhassib obtained the archive of Djekhy & Son, which contained many older papyri as well. When Muhassib heard that Eisenlohr and Krall had been seen in Karnak asking around for genuine antiquities—perhaps even papyri—he must have thought that these were good potential buyers. It is not unlikely that he packed all the papyri in his shop into the tin box, and that this is how the Ptolemaic papyrus that was to become P. Louvre E 7862 ended up with the archive, though not forming any part of it. There are even indications that on this day Muhassib had other Ptolemaic papyri on offer, one of which was bought by Eisenlohr (P. Louvre E 7862), the remainder by Jakob Krall. Any trace of the papyri Krall bought that day has vanished, with the possible exception of Papyrus Vienna 6052—the sale of a tomb from 239 BCE—which once formed part of the original lot offered by Muhammad Muhassib.

Between 675 and 572 BCE

The first known owner of the archive, the Theban choachyte Djekhy, makes his appearance on record in P. BM EA 10113, on 19 October 570 BCE. His son Iturech takes over the family business about 550 BCE, disappearing from view by 31 October 534 BCE at the latest. But the oldest papyrus from the archive of Djekhy & Son dates as far back as c. 675 BCE, and eleven other papyri were written during the reigns of Taharqa, Necho II, Psamtik II, and Apries (between 675 and 572 BCE). In other words, a substantial number of the papyri in the archive predate the archive itself.

Although the reason these older records are included is not completely clear, what we know is this: Many of these early (abnormal hieratic) papyri deal with choachytes and the leasing of land near Thebes, meaning that their subject matter alone already links them very closely to the archive proper. In Eisenlohr's days there was not a single Egyptologist who could read abnormal hieratic, nor would a dealer like

Muhammad Muhassib have had that skill; it is therefore highly unlikely that someone added this early, closely related group in modern times. The inevitable, albeit preliminary, conclusion is that for some reason these early papyri have been part of the Djekhy & Son archive since it was in actual use. By around 550 BCE, both men had become prominent among the Theban choachytes. As noted earlier, they were asked to safeguard possessions for clients, including a papyrus made out for a female choachyte friend. It is probably also not a coincidence that some of the official records of the Theban choachytes' association (P. Louvre E 7840 from 542–38 BCE) were found with the archive of Djekhy & Son. They were prominent, people asked them to safeguard their possessions and documents, and the old papyri could have come into the archive that way. Alternatively, because of their prominence, it is no coincidence that official records wound up in their archives and the old papyri are among those records.

There is another possible, and very simple, explanation for the fact that some material in the archive is older than the archivist: that Djekhy or Iturech inherited or acquired these documents through a family connection that, so many centuries later, we can no longer trace. In just this way will my son, born in 1999, eventually inherit the entire archive that went into creating our family tree, including nineteenth-century documents belonging to people with no obvious link to our family.

The papyri from the early group cover a period of roughly one hundred years. Three papyri—five contracts in all—are dated to the reign of Taharqa (690–664 BCE—P. Louvre E 7851, 7852, and 7856). Then there is a gap coinciding with the reign of Psamtik I between 664 and 610 BCE. It is a shame there are no documents dating from this turbulent period, both in Egypt as a whole and in Thebes itself. Psamtik I liberated Egypt from the Assyrians and soon managed to gain control of the whole country. In March 656 BCE he consolidated his hold on the south by forcing the Theban high priestess of Amun, Princess Shepenupet II (the daughter of Pye, also known to Egyptologists as Piankhy), to appoint his own daughter Nitocris as her heir-successor. In case any of the locals harbored doubts about this appointment, Psamtik sent Nitocris to Thebes along with a large fleet commanded by the great harbormaster Sematawytefnakht, a man who also plays a role in Papyrus Rylands 9 below.

During the subsequent reigns of Necho II, Psamtik II, and Apries, some new papyri were written that would eventually be deposited in the archive. This early group of papyri often mentions choachytes in connection with the leasing and tilling of land, like so many papyri from the archive proper.

The five contracts contained in P. Louvre E 7851, 7852, and 7856 from the reign of Taharqa mention six choachytes: Dyamunpankh, Hetepamun son of Dyamunpankh, Pamermesha son of Arenamun, Arenamun son of Heryesnef, and Ruruy son of Wennefer. As usual in Egypt, two of these choachytes had brought their sons into the business. Between c. 675 and 665 BCE these men leased some fields for tilling, a fact which came to light only in the late 1990s, when the abnormal hieratic contracts describing these business deals were published in the leading French journal *Revue d'Égyptologie*.

Although more than a hundred years would elapse between the last contract from the early group and the first land lease by the first known owner of the archive of Djekhy & Son, the common subject matter of both groups of papyri easily bridges the gap.

Just before Djekhy was born in 590 BCE, someone wrote P. Louvre E 7849, which was later to end up in the archive. It is a contract listing various marital property arrangements, but the people it mentions are otherwise unknown. Like P. Louvre E 7846, the contract setting out the maintenance to which Mrs. Tsendjehuty would be entitled in case of divorce (see chapter 1), this marital contract does not at first sight seem to belong to the archive. Seen in the context of the role Djekhy and his family played in safeguarding others' records, the presence in the archive of a marital contract is less unusual, particularly considering that a plan to divorce might provide a strong incentive for keeping such a contract outside the reach of one's spouse.

As noted in chapter 1, we know that the woman for whom the contract indexed as P. Louvre E 7846 was made came from a family with close business—and probably also friendly—ties with the family of Djekhy & Son. P. Louvre E 7846 was written by a priest of Amun and chief of priests of the second and fourth phyle (the monthly rotating priestly crew) of the temple of Montu, a man called Ip son of Montirtais. The scribe of P. Louvre E 7849 was Montirtais son of Ip: his father. Their handwriting is so similar[3] that it is reasonable to conclude that Ip had been trained by his father. It was common in ancient Egypt for sons to follow in their father's footsteps. Perhaps Djekhy's father Tesmontu already acted as a trustee for other people's documents. But in that case, why does the archive contain not a single document made for Tesmontu himself?

Between 570 and 534 BCE

The papyri from the archive of Djekhy & Son proper were all written during the reign of Pharaoh Amasis. The only exception is a papyrus from the British Museum, P. BM EA 10113, which does not really belong to the archive, but rather was kept with it for some time as a loan repayment guarantee. Between 570 and 534 BCE the documentary evidence is so complete that we can follow Djekhy & Son almost from year to year.

The archive tells us that Djekhy and Iturech not only brought funerary offerings, but also had a keen interest in agriculture. More than once, we see Djekhy together with business partners lease large flax fields. His son Iturech in turn leased out fields that had been given to him as the fee for his services to the deceased in the Theban necropolis. It would seem that he had extended the family business, going from tenant to landlord in a single generation.

The archive contains personal documents, business papers, and various contracts that are seemingly unrelated to the archive. Strictly speaking, the personal archive of Djekhy & Son contains fourteen documents: P. Louvre E 7861 (business conflict), 7855 (letter), 7848 (hostile takeover of a tomb), 7844 (land lease), 7847 (receipt), 7854 (official letter), 7842 (receipt), 7832 (purchase of a son), 7835 (receipt), 7838 (receipt), 7834 (receipt), 7836 (land lease), 7843 (business partnership), and 7839 (land lease). This is, admittedly, not much to work from if we want to understand the lives of people who lived 2,500 years ago. Fortunately, other documents do exist. Two papyri in the British Museum mention Djekhy: P. BM EA 10113 (loan) and 10432 (land lease). And the Egyptian Museum in Cairo has two papyri mentioning Djekhy's brother Rery: P. Caïro CG 30657 (business conflict) and 30665 (divorce), from which we can infer that Rery was unhappily married at least once in his life. It all looks surprisingly modern.

So many centuries later, some of the other papyri can only be tied to the archive using string and tape, despite having been deposited there; P. Louvre E 7841 (receipt) and 7850 (official letter) are among these. Some mention known business partners of Djekhy & Son, including P. Louvre E 7845A (land lease), 7845B (division of the harvest), 7846 (marital property arrangement), 7833 (land lease), and 7837 (land lease). P. Louvre E 7840 contains some of the official records of the Theban choachytes' association written between 542 and 538 BCE. They mention Iturech, his brother Khausenmin, and their uncle Rery.

Many papyri from the original Eisenlohr collection have been published in isolation since their acquisition by the Louvre in 1885—some very well, others rather badly. The papyri and their archivists have been known for some time in Egyptological circles. Until recently, however, the archive has largely been studied in fragments; nobody knew what it would yield if looked at as a whole.

The Saite Restoration

When Psamtik I succeeded to the throne of his father Necho in 664 BCE, he had control over Memphis and the city of Sais in the Delta. He quickly extended his hold on the Delta with the help of Greek and Carian mercenaries. At that time Egypt had already been a divided empire for centuries—the Delta region known as Lower Egypt and the south as Upper Egypt. Upper Egypt was ruled from Thebes by local strongmen like Montuemhat in collaboration with the priests of Amun and the Kushite pharaohs from Nubia. Within eight years, Psamtik I managed to reunify the empire, no doubt helped by the fact that he had kept the Assyrians definitely at bay in the east. Centuries of separate rule, however, meant that Upper and Lower Egypt had each developed different administrative management cultures, including independent administrative and legal formularies and even writing systems, with demotic used in Lower Egypt and what is now called abnormal hieratic in Upper Egypt.

Both writing systems had developed from the hieratic script used at the end of the New Kingdom, but somewhere along the line they had begun to diverge. The script used in the Delta is called early demotic to distinguish it from Ptolemaic and Roman demotic. The term 'abnormal hieratic' was coined in 1909 by the British Egyptologist Francis Llewellyn Griffith, who was fluent in early demotic and was to become the first scholar ever to properly publish abnormal hieratic texts. The best introduction to both scripts, including all aspects that set them apart from each other, is the article "La phase initiale du démotique ancien" by the Dutch demotist Sven Vleeming in the Belgian scientific journal *Chronique d'Égypte*.

Hieratic is a cursive script—mostly written in black and red ink on papyrus or on ostraca (pottery or limestone shards) in which the hieroglyphs are generally abbreviated to their most basic shape. Also, instead of drawing each sign or sign-group separately as in hieroglyphic writing, hieratic scribes tend to link signs through ligatures. As a rule of thumb one can say that as time progressed, hieratic drifted further and further away from its hieroglyphic origin. Old Kingdom hieratic is thus easier to read than cursive Ramesside hieratic. Hieratic allowed the scribes to write much more quickly than before. If we equate hieroglyphs with the printed letters of the Roman alphabet, hieratic would be those same letters written by hand. Abnormal hieratic would be shorthand.

The differences between these scripts can be seen from the ways *wah mu* (pronounced with a sharp h, and meaning 'pouring water,' or 'choachyte') is written. It looks accessible in hieroglyphs, and there is a clear difference between the abnormal hieratic version in P. Louvre E 7861 (middle) and its early demotic counterpart in P. Louvre E 7854 (bottom). The southern shorthand approached signs and sign-groups in a way that was quite distinct from the northern shorthand.

Figure 3. The difference between abnormal hieratic (middle) and early demotic (both scripts read from right to left) [Courtesy Musée du Louvre; author's facsimile]

Psamtik I and his successors from the Twenty-sixth or Saite Dynasty would have to build a new and loyal administrative system in Upper Egypt as quickly as possible, based on Delta traditions. This meant the whole legal system used in Upper Egypt up to that time, including the terminology used in courts and contracts, would have to go, as would the abnormal hieratic script. Within a few generations abnormal hieratic was erased in Thebes, to be replaced by the early demotic tradition from Lower Egypt and including a totally new and more abstract legal terminology. From the end of the reign of Amasis onward, all professional scribes in Egypt wrote early demotic. The last known line in abnormal hieratic is the signature of a witness—a Mr. Iufauamunip son of Iturech—on the back of P. Louvre E 7837 from 535 BCE.

The archive of Djekhy & Son allows us to follow this development almost on foot. Many of the documents in the archive were written by five scribes from the same family:

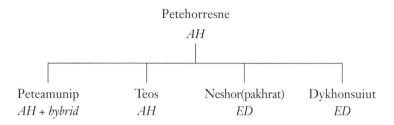

Petehorresne
AH

| Peteamunip | Teos | Neshor(pakhrat) | Dykhonsuiut |
| *AH + hybrid* | *AH* | *ED* | *ED* |

AH: abnormal hieratic; *ED*: early demotic

These scribes called themselves overseers of the necropolis—literally translated, 'overseers of the desert.' Apart from choachytes like Djekhy, the necropolis teemed with embalmers, mourners, priests, tourists, pickpockets, undertakers, and craftsmen, meaning that some degree of management was required. Importing a mummy into this area was subject to taxation, and that tax was paid to the overseer of the necropolis. The overseers also wrote official contracts, some of which wound up in the archive of Djekhy & Son. Sometimes they moonlighted in real estate.

P. Louvre E 7128 is a sale from 511 BCE, the twelfth regnal year of Darius I. In this contract, the overseer of the necropolis Chayutayudeny son of Peteamunip declares to the choachyte Psenese son of Heryrem that he has received the money for a plot on which to build a house. But this was not just any plot of land. It was located somewhere in the precinct of the tomb of Pharaoh Osorkon. This same royal tomb is mentioned again in the abnormal hieratic P. Louvre E 7858 (609 BCE)—a donation of land kept in the archive of Djekhy & Son—and in P. Turin 2123 (512 BCE), written nearly a hundred years later. Apparently this tomb of Osorkon was a landmark in the Theban necropolis. Parts of it were also for sale. The overseers of the necropolis were indispensable for those who wanted to get things done on the west bank of the Nile.

Memphis had its own overseers of the necropolis who, like their The-ban counterparts, also appear to have embarked on lucrative real estate deals. Stela Louvre C. 101 was made in regnal year 8 of Psamtik I. It is a small limestone stela measuring forty-one by twenty-eight centimeters.

It was found by the French archaeologist Auguste Mariette during his extensive excavations at Saqqara between 1849 and 1852. The text was cut out in rather ugly hieratic, but some of the terminology in the text itself—a stone copy of a contract of sale—is undoubtedly early demotic. From this we can infer that demotic had already reached Memphis during the first reigning years of Psamtik I. This makes Stela Louvre C. 101 a true highlight on the long road toward the supplanting of abnormal hieratic by demotic. The text was published by the famous (and brilliant) demotist Michel Malinine:

> Regnal year 8, second month of the akhet season under Pharaoh Psamtik, may he live forever. The overseer of the necropolis Kayrau son of Ptahhotep has said to the washerman Peteamunip son of Pakem: "You have satisfied my heart with the price for this tomb that is located in the mountain of Anubis, that was made by the necropolis workman Pamy son of Nesptah. Its south is the tomb that belongs to the choachyte Ipy, the tomb of the salesman Payuyuhor being between them. Its north is the tomb of the salesman Patjenef. Its east is the tomb that belongs to the carpenter Maakhonsu son of NN. Its west is the tomb of the choachyte Hor son of Iby. (This tomb, it is) yours from regnal year 8, second month of the peret season onwards." In the handwriting of NN.

Table 3. Overseers of the necropolis mentioned in the Djekhy & Son archive

Scribe	Script	Papyrus	Year BCE
Petehorresne	Abnormal hieratic	Louvre E 7861	568
	Abnormal hieratic	Louvre E 7848	559
	Abnormal hieratic	Louvre E 7847	552
Peteamunip	Abnormal hieratic	BM EA 10432	556
	Abnormal hieratic	Louvre E 7845B	after 554
	Abnormal hieratic	Louvre E 7847 (W)	552
	Hybrid	Caïro 30567	547
Teos	Abnormal hieratic	Caïro 30665	544
Neshor(pakhrat)	Early demotic	Louvre E 7836	536
	Early demotic	Louvre E 7839	534
Dykhonsuiut	Early demotic	Louvre E 7836 (W)	536

W: scribe signing a document as a witness

The overseers of the necropolis were men of great influence. In the archive of Djekhy & Son they mostly appear as notary scribes of official contracts (see Table 3).

P. Louvre E 7861 is the first document written by Petehorresne son of Peteamunip, the earliest ancestor in the family tree above, which extended well into the time of the Persian rulers. P. Louvre E 7861 is heavily damaged at the bottom so that the name of the scribe is lost. There are also two vertical oblong abrasions where the ink has disappeared in a number of lines. Comparing the text to documents written at the same time, however, suggests strongly that P. Louvre E 7861 was written by Petehorresne. The first scientific publication by Michel Malinine did not address this issue. The name Petehorresne ('Who was given by Horus of Resen') is believed to originate from a Saite cult in the Delta that was probably brought to Upper Egypt in the entourage of Nitocris. This etymology suggests that Petehorresne's Theban father may have decided that it would be politically advantageous to name his son after some influential official from the Delta.

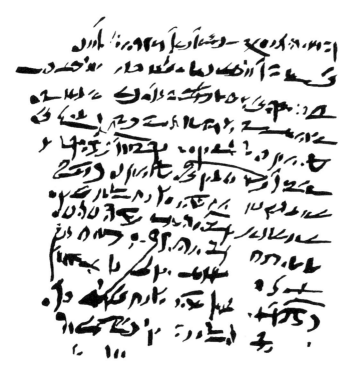

Figure 4. P. Louvre E 7861 [Courtesy Musée du Louvre; author's facsimile][4]

When Petehorresne wrote the abnormal hieratic P. Louvre E 7861 in 568 BCE, the rise of demotic—probably as part of a conscious Saite restoration policy—had been going on for decades. Indeed, Petehorresne's style in this papyrus already shows some early demotic traits. The four witnesses countersigning the contract, for instance, signed on the back of the papyrus exactly opposite the beginning of the official declaration starting with *djed (NN)*, '(NN) has said,' which is the first sign group at the beginning of line 2 on the front of the papyrus (figures 4 and 5). This is the way early demotic Egyptian scribes indicated that these four witnesses had actually been present when the oral declaration was made. The theory is that the Egyptian scribe, after he wrote the contract, put his finger on the beginning of the statement on the front, and then made a small mark on the back (where he could see the dent made by his finger) to indicate where the witnesses had to sign, thus symbolizing that these witnesses had actually been present when the oral statement about the affair was made (see figure 5). This mark on the back is not always there. It would have been just as easy for a professional scribe to point with his finger at the spot where the witnesses had to sign. Except in the slightly earlier Papyrus BM EA 10113 (570 BCE), this graphical trick never occurs in the abnormal hieratic legal tradition. Witnesses to a standard abnormal hieratic contract always signed on the front of the papyrus, below and to the side of the text itself. Apparently this was a neat early demotic trick that had attracted the attention of Petehorresne and was incorporated into his own style.

Figure 5. Position of the name of the first witness on the back of P. Louvre E 7861 in relation to *djed (NN)*, '(NN) has said,' at the beginning of line 2 on the front of the papyrus, *djed (NN)* shown here in mirror image [Courtesy Musée du Louvre; author's facsimile]

Another early demotic element in P. Louvre E 7861 is the opening statement by party A to party B: *dyek meter haty*, 'You have satisfied my heart,' at the beginning of line 10. About sixteen years later, Petehorresne would use this early demotic legal formula once again in P. Louvre E 7847 (552 BCE). He also taught it to his son Peteamunip, who used it in P. Caïro CG 30657 (547 BCE). Thus a single early demotic legal formula was adopted by a family of Theban scribes using abnormal hieratic.

It is worth noting that these insights are based on what is certainly a tiny fraction of the work generated by the scribes in question. We know that Petehorresne was active between 568 and 552 BCE. If we assume that he wrote only two documents a week, in his sixteen-year career he would have produced 1,664 documents, of which only three are left (less than 0.2 percent). If Petehorresne actually wrote two documents a day for 200 out of 365 days, he would have written 6,400 documents, the three preserved papyri representing less than 0.05 percent.

The case of the scribe Peteamunip is a story in itself. We can infer that he worked at the office of his father Petehorresne, at least from time to time. The archive of Djekhy & Son contains one document that was written by Petehorresne in 552 BCE and then countersigned by Peteamunip (P. Louvre E 7847). As can be seen from some older traces in the left lower corner of the papyrus, Petehorresne cut off a piece from an old account, wiped it clean, and then turned it ninety degrees to the left before he started to write. The ancient Egyptian scribes liked to recycle.

At the end of the contract, however, something went wrong. There was no room left on the last line (line 8) for the final word of the actual contract—'remainder, rest,' which looks like a 3 turned 90 degrees to the left with a dot above it. Instead, Petehorresne wrote it in the next line immediately before his own signature.

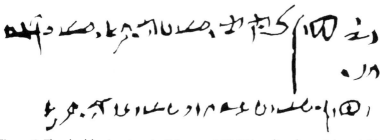

Figure 6. The double signature in P. Louvre E 7847 (reading from right to left): "remainder. In the handwriting of the overseer of the necropolis Petehorresne <son of> Peteamunip. In the handwriting of Peteamunip son of Petehorresne" [Courtesy Musée du Louvre; author's facsimile]

Apparently this was enough to distract him, because he then forgot to write 'son of' after his own name (in accordance with the convention in demotic, this has been added between < > in the translation above to indicate that something was forgotten). To make matters worse, the result of fixing this mistake was that the last part of his father's name—the house sign in the element 'Ip' in Peteamunip—now no longer fit on the line. It looks like an upturned 'V' followed by a vertical stroke and a dot. Very annoying for any professional scribe! So the house sign too was pushed to the next line.

Curiously, and we have no idea why, Petehorresne wrote the element 'Amun' in 'Peteamunip' (his father's name) in early demotic, whereas his son Peteamunip wrote the 'Amun' element in his own name in abnormal hieratic. It is as if I were to write 'rode vis' (red fish) in modern Dutch while my teenage son used the archaic 1920s spelling 'roode visch.' Whatever the reason for this discrepancy, Peteamunip's signature suggests that he began his career as a scribe of abnormal hieratic.

The name of the scribe of P. BM EA 10432, one of the texts from the British Museum that mentions Djekhy son of Tesmontu, is unfortunately unknown because the bottom of the papyrus has broken off. The handwriting, however, shows enough similarities to other contracts of this period that we can infer it to have been written by Peteamunip son of Petehorresne.

P. BM EA 10432 is an abnormal hieratic land lease from 556 BCE. But the crucial term to denote 'lease' in this papyrus is the early demotic verb *sehen* (pronounced with a sharp h, meaning 'entrust, commission'), which was to replace the various sometimes cumbersome abnormal hieratic phrases to describe a lease: *dy (er seka)*, 'give (to till),' or *shep (er seka)*, 'receive (to till).' This is one of the more famous examples showing how a single early demotic abstract legal formula could make all abnormal hieratic renderings superfluous. It is interesting to note, however, that the verb *sehen* also appears in official administrative sources from Deir al-Medina dating mostly from the Nineteenth and Twentieth Dynasties (1307–1070 BCE). This suggests that the demotic term had been used by Theban officials in the same sense hundreds of years before it reappeared following Psamtik's reunification of Egypt. It is true that in living languages words are apt to fall into disuse within a relatively short period of time, and perhaps that is what happened here. After the official administration connected with the work on the royal tombs came to an end in the late New Kingdom, perhaps Theban officials no longer had any need of such a term.

While Peteamunip may have started his career as a scribe of abnormal hieratic, like his father Petehorresne (who wrote the abnormal hieratic P. Louvre E 7861, 7848, and 7847), he paid close attention to contemporaneous early demotic texts and incorporated useful elements into his own style. P. Louvre E 7845B (after 554 BCE) was also written by Peteamunip. Although only a fragment of this text remains, it clearly shows that his roots lay in abnormal hieratic. Since Peteamunip, his father, and his brothers all worked as scribes—one brother trained in abnormal hieratic, two younger brothers writing early demotic (see above, "The Saite Restoration")—one can imagine family conversations about the evolution of the craft and the finer points of these competing writing systems.

One fine day in spring or early summer of the year 547 BCE, the choachyte Petedjehuty son of Inaros left some possessions with Djekhy's brother Rery for safekeeping. Petedjehuty is also known from a business quarrel with Djekhy in September 559 BCE, over choachytes' rights to a tomb. But the Theban choachytes formed a close-knit community; it was inevitable that clashes would arise in the course of doing business. Any conflict between them was likely to be solved through the Theban choachytes' association, not through a legal court. Apparently Rery had stored some of Petedjehuty's possessions with his mother Khausenese. That is one version of the story. It could also be that Petedjehuty had delivered or lent something to Khausenese and had not been paid for this. It all depends how we choose to interpret the crux of this text:[5]

> Regnal year 24, second month of the peret season under Pharaoh l.p.h. Amasis l.p.h. The choachyte Petedjehuty son of Inaros has said to the choachyte Rery son of Tesmontu: "You have satisfied my heart with all the things of which I have said to you: 'They are with Mrs. Khausenese, your mother.' I am far (?) from you as far as these things are concerned. No son or daughter of mine will be able to come to you on account of them. My heart is satisfied with it." In the handwriting of Peteamunip son of Petehorresne, the overseer of the necropolis.

The key sentence is: "They are with Mrs. Khausenese, your mother." Does this mean that these possessions—the 'things' to which Petedjehuty refers—had been physically present in the house of Mrs. Khausenese? Or is this an abbreviated or garbled variant of a formula known from early demotic loans to indicate that Petedjehuty had a claim on Mrs. Khausenese? There are arguments for and against each interpretation, but these do not concern us here, and neither does the question of whether someone else from Djekhy & Son was present that day. What does concern us is Peteamunip's handwriting in P. Caïro CG 30657.

We know that Peteamunip had been trained as a scribe in the local abnormal hieratic writing tradition and that, like his father Petehorresne, he incorporated some tricks from early demotic into his own style. P. Caïro CG 30657 is interesting in that it has confounded even specialists for years: no one has been able to decide whether P. Caïro CG 30657 belongs to the abnormal hieratic or early demotic scribal tradition. In fact, this is a typical example of the limitations of our own minds, a phenomenon also known as tunnel vision, because P. Caïro CG 30657 is simply a hybrid, with one foot firmly planted in each writing system. "The best of both worlds," the English call it. Apparently Peteamunip's style had developed from pure abnormal hieratic into a hybrid script, showing that the transition toward early demotic in this specific case was a conscious and individual decision by a single Theban scribe.

3

Trust
Djekhy 570–549 BCE

Just a Businessman from Thebes

19 October 570 BCE (Papyrus BM EA 10113)

Papyrus BM EA 10113 is the first official document mentioning Djekhy son of Tesmontu. It is a contract in which Djekhy's debtor promises to repay a sum of money within a specified time. Djekhy may have been twenty-something at the time. Papyrus BM EA 10113 was sold in March 1837 during an auction of the collection of Giovanni d'Athanasi by Leigh Sotheby. This papyrus was only kept in the archive of Djekhy & Son for the short duration of the loan. After the loan was repaid, it would be returned to the debtor as proof of payment.

The loan is dated to regnal year 20, second month of the shemu season[1] of Pharaoh Apries. It is also the last known reference to Apries, who was overthrown by his general Amasis. Ironically, Apries had ordered Amasis to put down a revolt by native soldiers (the Egyptian army at that time consisted of Greek mercenaries and the native, or actually Libyan, warrior class of the machimoi). Rather than quelling the revolt, however, Amasis threw in his lot with the mutineers. They proclaimed him king in 570 BCE. In the battle of Momemphis, about halfway between Sais and Memphis, Amasis vanquished Apries's army of thirty thousand Carians and Ionians. Apries fled. In 567 BCE he attempted to regain power, but despite support from a Babylonian army, this time Apries lost for good. Amasis, somewhat against his will, put his rival at the disposal of the mob. Apries was lynched, and Amasis buried him with honors in Sais.

Turning back to our document: While Egyptians in some parts of the country had recognized Amasis as the new king in 570 BCE, the scribe of

P. BM EA 10113 was not among them. This may mean Amasis had not yet gained full control of Thebes by the time the document was written.

Horkhonsu son of Ituru, the scribe, is otherwise unknown. He wrote in a curious mix of local Theban abnormal hieratic and early demotic imported from the Delta. He was originally trained in Thebes, but was evidently also learning early demotic to keep up with the competition. Scribes were wont to do work for private clients, offering their services to people passing through temple courts, and one supposes the demand for contracts written in early demotic was growing by this time.

What kind of a person was this new king Amasis? The Greek journalist-chronicler Herodotus (c. 485–425 BCE) apparently liked him, as suggested by his description of Amasis below. When Herodotus traveled through Egypt and talked to the people about Amasis, he may have encountered people who could tell him stories about the king that they had heard from their parents and grandparents, but only just, in view of life expectancy at that time:

> When Apries was thus driven out, Amasis became king. He came from the district of Sais and the city of Syuf. The Egyptians first despised Amasis, thinking rather poorly of him, because he was a man of the people and did not come from a distinguished family. After some time, however, he won their sympathy through wisdom, not because he was stubborn. Among the countless precious possessions he had there was also a footbath made of gold. Amasis and his guests always used it to wash their feet. He had it smashed to pieces and from these he had a divine statue made. He placed this at a convenient spot in town and the Egyptians kept coming to see the statue, showering it with honor. When Amasis heard what they had done, he summoned the Egyptians and told them that the statue had been made from the footbath the Egyptians used to vomit and pee in, and to wash their feet, and now they showered it with honor. And this, he told them, is what had happened to him as well, just like the footbath. Even though he had been a common man before, he was now their king and he asked them to honor and respect him accordingly. This way he won the hearts of the Egyptians, so that they agreed to become his subjects. . . .
>
> He always did as follows. In the early morning, when the market would start to become crowded, he dutifully dealt with all the affairs that were presented to him. Afterwards, however, he spent his time

drinking and making fun with his mates, being rather lighthearted and playful. His friends were not amused at all because of this and they reproached him, saying: "King, your conduct is not becoming, debasing yourself with foolish behavior. You should sit in a stately manner on a grand throne and handle your affairs. This would give the Egyptians the idea that they are ruled by a great man and it would do much for your image. The way it is now you are not behaving in a royal fashion." And he answered: "The owners of handbows will strain them the moment they want to use them. Once they're done with them, they will loosen them again, because they would break if they were to be kept tightly stretched. This is also the case with man. If he is always serious and does not relax through sports regularly, he will become either mad or dull. Because I know this so well, I divide my time between both ways to approach life."

P. BM EA 10113, a contract laying down the terms for the repayment of a loan, was made for Djekhy. In this document, the embalmer Hepy son of Teos states that he has received one deben of silver from Djekhy, about ninety-one grams, measured in accordance with the standard of the Treasury of Thebes. This is the approximate weight. The actual deben weights that have been preserved differ slightly, but this is a common phenomenon. The same applies, for instance, to the pound in seventeenth-century Holland. This was derived from the Roman weight system, but there was also an Amsterdam pound of about 494 grams, a Hague pound of about 470 grams, a medicinal-scientific pound weighing 369 grams, and the French livre of 490 grams.

Since Hepy was an embalmer and Djekhy a choachyte, it is tempting to assume that these men knew each other well, something that is also suggested by the amount of the loan. One deben of silver would buy one-third of a slave. To ensure nobody would tamper with the figures, the amount was repeated in fractions.

Apart from this contract, Hepy is unknown. His name, 'Apis has come,' may mean that he was born in Memphis, home of the holy Apis bull. In the light of the reforms initiated by the Saite pharaohs, comprising the entire internal administration of the country, this would not be surprising. Many people from Lower Egypt would have been posted in Thebes to manage government affairs or may have moved there because of job opportunities. But we know so little about Hepy that the best we can do is surmise.

At first sight P. BM EA 10113 is an ordinary loan. From Hepy's statement, we know the loan was for seven months, and repayment was due in the fourth month of the akhet season of regnal year 21—between 12 April and 12 May 569 BCE. For each month that Hepy did not pay, interest would accrue at a rate of one-third of a kite per deben of silver (one deben being ten kite). It was a secured loan, with virtually all of Hepy's possessions acting as security, including his children:

> They (the capital sum plus interest) will be on my head regarding the securities you will require from me, whichever one, be it house, male servant, female servant, son, daughter, silver, copper, clothing, oil, emmer, or whatever in this world.

To offer your own child as security for a loan appears, and indeed is, rather brutal. But the practice has been recorded as late as 2009, when a man in the Kemerovo District in Siberia refused to give up a one-and-a-half-year-old boy during a police raid on his house, claiming the boy had been given to him as security for a loan. And in some parts of the world, bonded labor by children still serves to secure a loan. Whatever the case today, in Hepy's time such terms were acceptable. And yet there is something unusual about this loan.

It appears that if Hepy repaid the loan within the seven-month deadline, no interest would be owed. We know enough about Djekhy to infer that he was a successful businessman, which casts doubt on the idea that he would have granted an interest-free loan. It seems more probable that the amount Hepy actually received was less than one deben of silver, and that the amount cited in the contract was in fact the capital sum plus interest. This arrangement is not uncommon in loans from the Ptolemaic Period, which supports the suggestion that it may apply here in P. BM EA 10113. While this loan is a relatively minor part of Djekhy's history, it does show that he was affluent enough to lend a sizable sum of money to someone else in the midst of civil war and great uncertainty.

The loan contract was signed by two witnesses. The first of these was Teos son of Khonsuirau—another good Theban name that also appears in records of the Theban choachytes' association (P. Louvre E 7840) made some thirty years later, in about 540 BCE. These official records were found with the archive of Djekhy & Son and were probably deposited there by Iturech. From his presence in these records, we can conclude that the

Teos son of Khonsuirau mentioned in 540 BCE was also a choachyte. It is possible, but not very likely, that the name in these documents thirty years apart refers to the same man—if, for instance, Teos was about twenty years old in 570 BCE, he might still have been working thirty years later. It is more likely that these references are to two different people, and that they are grandfather and grandson. Ancient Egyptians often named their children after their parents, and it was customary for children—especially sons—to succeed their fathers in their work. It follows that if the later Teos was a choachyte and the other man was indeed his grandfather, he may well have been a choachyte himself, maybe even a friend of Djekhy son of Tesmontu.

The second witness is called Ptahirtais son of Efau. He appears again in a legal document from 568 BCE absolving Djekhy from a claim (P. Louvre E 7861), also as a witness on Djekhy's behalf.

It appears therefore that both witnesses to P. BM EA 10113 had a closer relationship to Djekhy than we can tell from their signatures alone. This makes sense. Djekhy was lending a considerable amount of money; it would be reasonable to do so in the presence of witnesses he knew and trusted.

Trustee

27 October 568 BCE (Papyrus Louvre E 7861)
Djekhy did not act only as a choachyte. We know this from his business enterprises, but also from the fact that people regularly asked Djekhy & Son to act as a trustee. We have seen this already in the case of the marital contract written for Mrs. Tsendjehuty, the daughter of Djekhy's business partner Teos son of Amunirtais (P. Louvre E 7846; see ch. 1). It is possible that the actual trustee in that case was in fact Djekhy's son Iturech.

But even in the most successful businesses things occasionally go wrong. This happened to Djekhy in 569 or 568 BCE. A man called Wesirtais son of Teos and Mutirtais—perhaps a son of Djekhy's business partner Teos, although we know nothing about him beyond the information in the Djekhy & Son archive—had apparently deposited some possessions with Djekhy or had some sort of claim on him. But when Wesirtais came to retrieve these items, Djekhy no longer had them. The protocol of this case is now kept in Paris as the abnormal hieratic P. Louvre E 7861 (see figure 4). Although the bottom of the text containing the name of the scribe has broken off, we know it was written by the overseer of the necropolis Petehorresne son of Peteamunip. He comes from the family of scribes mentioned earlier (see above, "The Saite Restoration"). There were four witnesses present when P. Louvre E 7861 was written. They all signed on the back of the papyrus, directly opposite the beginning of the official statement *djed NN* ('NN has said') on the front.

Unfortunately, the protocol is not very clear about what happened. This is how Petehorresne wrote it down 2,500 years ago:

> I (i.e., the claimant Wesirtais) have come to you about the seven possessions you had, whereas you say: "They were already taken." You took an oath for me in the presence of Khonsuemwasneferhotep, saying: "They were already taken." For this reason I no longer have a claim on you from today onward. . . . You have satisfied my heart with the oath in the presence of Khonsuemwasneferhotep, starting today.

Twenty-five centuries ago, taking an oath in the presence of a deity—in a society in which religion was a fundamental part of life—was a serious undertaking, not to be made lightly. This did not stop unscrupulous ancient Egyptians—including Amasis himself, as we will soon see—from taking false oaths, but there was a great deal at stake for Djekhy. The entire local choachytes' association—a small, tight-knit community in which all the members knew or were related to one another—would have been watching over his shoulder on that October day in 568 BCE. Taking a false oath could well ruin his reputation as a trustee.

The ancient Egyptian business of oracles and divine judgment formed an easy source of income for the temples, and could even be described as a soul-saving industry. Not everyone was impressed. According to Herodotus, Pharaoh Amasis, who came from a humble family, had developed his own view of the Egyptian oracle industry that stemmed from his own wild youth:

> It is said about Amasis that he, when he was still a private person, was rather keen on drinking and having fun, not taking life too seriously. The moment he became broke due to his life of drinking and luxury, he would simply steal his money for maintenance wherever he could. The people he had stolen from would file a complaint against him, and if he denied the charges, this often brought him before a divine oracle, if there was one. He was often convicted by these oracles, but just as often set free. When he became king he did the following. As to the many

gods that had acquitted him, saying that he was not a thief, he did not look after their temples and did not present any gifts to embellish them, and did not even visit them to bring offerings, because he thought they were worthless with their lying oracles. The many gods who had convicted him as a thief were much honored by him, as he considered them to be the true gods, because they had oracles that didn't lie.

P. Louvre E 7861 actually mentions two oaths. Djekhy's oath before Khonsuemwasneferhotep was taken with regard to the 'missing' possessions of Wesirtais. The second oath was taken by Wesirtais before Amun and Pharaoh, stating that he was satisfied with the way the affair had been handled. This kind of oath before Amun and Pharaoh was a standard component of abnormal hieratic legal documents. But with the rise of early demotic in Thebes in the wake of the Saite policy reformers, the oath before Amun and Pharaoh vanished from legal contracts. The early demotic tradition had its own legal formulae that left no room for a Theban deity like Amun, although it is unknown whether this reform was part of a conscious policy to stamp out the influence of Amun in the region.

The oath taken by Djekhy before Khonsuemwasneferhotep arose more often among the Theban choachytes. In 559 BCE Djekhy and his partners managed to prevent a hostile takeover of a tomb, forcing their legal adversary to take an oath before the same god. Petehorresne son of Peteamunip was the scribe who recorded that transaction as well (P. Louvre E 7848), and went so far as to note that the oath should be taken on the day of a full moon, which is when the power of the lunar god Khonsuemwasneferhotep would be strongest. It is likely that the day on which Djekhy took the oath referred to in P. Louvre E 7861 was also a full moon day. It would have given Wesirtais more confidence that Djekhy spoke the truth. Where Djekhy took this oath is not recorded, but the most likely location would be the temple of Khonsuemwasneferhotep in the southwest corner of the large complex of Amun in Thebes. What we do know is that Djekhy & Son always carefully kept the quitclaim that was written (P. Louvre E 7861) to close the case of the 'missing' possessions of Wesirtais.

Demotic Temple Oaths

Even if the oath before Amun and Pharaoh in legal contracts vanished with the demise of abnormal hieratic in Thebes, the oath before the god stayed on as a legal instrument. A large number of so-called temple oaths written on ostraca have been found, dating from the Ptolemaic Period. They deal mostly with everyday issues like theft, adultery, failure to pay, and so on. The temple oaths allow us a refreshing look into the actual lives of the ancient Egyptians, not the idealized autobiographies inscribed on tomb walls.

Many of these oaths were published by the German demotist Ursula Kaplony-Heckel in her book *Die demotischen Tempeleide* (1963). Although we have learned much more about the temple oaths since then, her pioneering effort remains impressive. Ostracon Bodleian Library 1279, now in the Ashmolean Museum in Oxford, is a temple oath from the Ptolemaic Period (no. 123 from the Kaplony-Heckel catalogue):

> Copy of the oath that Psenkhonsu son of NN will have to take in the temple of Khonsu Lord of Lifetime, in regnal year 5, fourth month of the akhet season, on behalf of Amuniu son of NN, saying: "As Khonsu lives, the Lord of Lifetime who resides here, and those living here with him. As far as this grain is concerned, an earthenware pot and the piece of clothing you have come to argue with me about. I didn't take them away and I didn't have them taken away. I don't know anyone who took them away and no profit from it reached me. There is no lying in this oath." If he takes this oath, then [he] must [leave him alone. If he does not take the oath], he will have to reimburse (?) them. The oath was [. . .] taken [. . .] the servant.

The actual content of O. Bodleian Library 1279 may have been very similar to the oath taken by Djekhy in October 568 BCE, so in a sense nothing really changed when the oath before Amun and Pharaoh was deleted from the early demotic contracts from Thebes. If there was a conflict, the ancient Egyptians would seek the services of any court, be it of this world or the next.

A Letter from the North

16 February 559 BCE (Papyrus Louvre E 7855)

Following the incident with Wesirtais in 568 BCE, the archive of Djekhy & Son is silent for about ten years. This silence does not necessarily reflect a lack of work during this time. It was a period of great political upheavals and uncertainty. Cambyses I of Persia had just died and was succeeded by his son, who would become known as Cyrus the Great. Solon, the famous lawmaker of Athens, had also died. Plato records that Solon had visited Egypt some years before his death and in Sais had been told by a local priest that the stories about Atlantis were all true. Apparently even in those days, tourist touts regaled unsuspecting visitors with tall tales. And Herodotus tells us that during this period Amasis restored Egypt to its former glory:

> They say that during the reign of Amasis Egypt blossomed as never before as to what comes to the land from the river and what comes from the land to the inhabitants, and that in this time there were no less than twenty thousand inhabited places. It was Amasis who decreed that each Egyptian had to make an annual statement to the head of the district where he lived about the way he made a living. If a man didn't do this or could not make a statement about an honest way to make a living, he would be punished by death. Solon of Athens took over this law from Egypt and issued it to the people of Athens. They have always abided by it, because this is a law that nobody can find fault with.

The year 559 BCE also saw the introduction of standardized coinage by Croesus of Lydia, although neither this nor subjugating a number of Greek cities was enough to keep Cyrus the Great of Persia from conquering Lydia in 547 BCE. We may take it that Djekhy heard about some of these events in due course. But the ten-year gap in the archive may be explained simply by a busy household. In this period Djekhy's wife Ituru gave birth to at least two sons and probably more. It is safe to say that some of these children would die long before their time, and although child mortality was a fact of life in ancient Egypt, this must have affected Ituru and her husband. Moreover, all the details that make up human life—from caring for children or aging parents to going to the choachytes' pub around the corner to exchange the latest gossip from the Theban choachytes' community—we know absolutely nothing about. Still, it is not difficult to imagine that Djekhy's household during this period was quite hectic, especially if it also included Ituru's ailing father and Djekhy's grumpy mother. In ancient Egypt, your children were your pension.

These ten years could also have been a time during which Djekhy built up his business, which in ancient Egypt would have been a family business to be carried on by his children.

We must, however, keep in mind that only about twenty papyri remain to document Djekhy's life. Many have probably been lost or destroyed over time. Reconstructing his life from this fragmentary record is almost like reconstructing a modern life 2,500 years later on the basis of a single agenda from 2011. One would very much like to know what Djekhy did in these years to build a future for his wife Ituru and their children.

On 16 February 559 BCE, an unknown Mr. Djefmin wrote a letter to an equally unknown Mrs. Mutirtais. It so happens that P. Louvre E 7861 from 568 BCE also mentions a woman called Mutirtais. The natural thing would be to assume that these are references to the same woman, but this is far from certain; Mutirtais is a common Theban name.

The woman Mutirtais who received this letter by Djefmin is not the only addressee. The letter was in fact explicitly addressed to the choachyte Djekhy, suggesting some degree of intimacy between him and the sender. It also shows that Djefmin held Djekhy responsible for the well-being of Mutirtais.

We do know this: In 560 or 559 BCE Djefmin, who wrote the letter, and Djekhy left Thebes to go north, maybe on a business trip. Djekhy then returned home. We can assume that Djekhy was asked by Djefmin—who was staying behind in the north—to take good care of Mrs. Mutirtais, but the tone of the letter suggests that Djefmin remained anxious. February was a cold month; the temperature could drop below eight degrees Celsius at night. This may have contributed to Djefmin's anxiety and prompted him to write to Mrs. Mutirtais. The letter is addressed to "the choachyte Djekhy son of Tesmontu, from Djefmin," suggesting that Mutirtais read only a little, or not at all. The tone of voice easily closes the 2,500-year gap between us and the ancient Egyptians:

Djefmin greets Mrs. Mutirtais. May she live! I have had wheat (?) brought to you, (to be precise) one sack (measured with the oipe) of forty hin, from the hilly field of Djekhy son of Nadjedkara. However, you haven't written to say that it has been brought to you. May she live! I have had Psamtikdyneheh bring you a hin pot of honey. I have had the shrine-opener of the temple of Amun, Teos son of Pasematawy, bring you a sack and an oipe of emmer (measured with the oipe) of forty hin, and an additional ten (bundles of) flax. Let there be written to me that they have reached you. Anything you want, if you tell

Djekhy son of Tesmontu, "This is something that I need more often," then I will make sure it will be brought to him.

Djefmin greets Djekhy son of Tesmontu. May he live! You haven't written to me since you went south. May he live! Let care be taken of Mrs. Mutirtais. Make sure she has all she needs. Anything that you will give her is something she needs more often. Let care also be taken of this little boy that is with you. Written by Djefmin in regnal year 12, second month of the akhet season, (day) 18.

About 170 liters of wheat and emmer, half a liter of honey, ten bundles of flax, and a letter to the choachyte Djekhy. Djefmin's clear concern for Mutirtais and the little boy suggests she was either his mother or his wife, and the little boy was his little brother or his son. Djefmin made it very clear to Mutirtais that he had had all sorts of commodities sent to her, and chided her for not showing the expected gratitude. This point made, he made sure Mutirtais also knew that Djekhy would be there to support her if there was any trouble. Apart from a tiny reproach that Djekhy might have dropped him a line or two, all Djefmin really wanted was to ensure that someone would take care of both Mutirtais and the little boy, perhaps staying in Djekhy's home. The quickest way to achieve this was by this letter to his friend, or even perhaps his relative, Djekhy.

Working with Papyri
The first scientific edition of P. Louvre E 7855 was published by an American demotist in 1985. This edition was based on the heliogravure of the text as it appeared in the original publication by August Eisenlohr and Eugène Revillout, *Corpus Papyrorum Aegypti*, published between 1885 and 1902. It appears that the author never checked the original papyrus to ensure that his rendering of the text was correct and that he had not mistaken imperfections or accidental marks on the original for ink in the photograph. Such meticulousness costs time and money, but is essential to prevent mistakes in translation.

In the case of P. Louvre E 7855 this oversight caused at least one major mistake. In this first edition—or *editio princeps*, as it is called—Djekhy sent Djefmin to the south. The American author read: "making that I (Djefmin) went south, that you (Djekhy) did" instead of "going south that you (Djekhy) did," which is the literal and rather long-winded ancient Egyptian formulation. It looks like a rather innocent mistake, but it does introduce a serious uncertainty: did Djefmin go south or was it Djekhy?

What the American author read as the early demotic sign for 'making' on the photograph in Revillout and Eisenlohr's original publication looks like a correction below the line that was added later by Djefmin, if he was indeed the author of the letter. Early demotic corrections, however, are usually written above the line, and it turns out that the early demotic sign for 'making' was never actually there. Raising the original P. Louvre E 7855 to the light makes it clear that what the American demotist assumed was a written mark is actually a hole shaped exactly like the early demotic sign for 'making.' The photograph published by Eisenlohr and Revillout was taken against a dark background, so that the hole appears to be ink. This is just one example of the kinds of mistakes that can creep in through lazy scholarship.

Marital Property Arrangement
7 November 549 BCE (Papyrus Louvre E 7846)
It had long been been unclear why the contract written on the occasion of the marriage of Mrs. Tsendjehuty, the daughter of the choachyte Teos and Mrs. Ruru, to the choachyte Iturech son of Petiese was found in the archive of Djekhy & Son. We now know that the families of Teos and Djekhy were close business partners and that Djekhy was a prominent man in the local Theban choachyte community. But let us go back to the beginning.

On 7 November 549 BCE the choachyte Iturech knocked at the door of his colleague Teos. This appears at first sight to be the usual overture to a wedding in Saite Egypt. The bridegroom knocks at the door with a dowry, he makes an oral statement, a contract is made to arrange the marital property, and the whole village turns up for the party. This time, however, there was more to the story than meets the eye. Seven years earlier, in 556 BCE, Iturech and Tsendjehuty had already been married.

The marital property contract P. Louvre E 7846 was written in abnormal hieratic, the local Theban script. This means the wedding was concluded according to Theban law, in line with the use of that script. Some of the legal formulae used in this contract can be traced directly back to the so-called Ramesside Adoption Papyrus written centuries earlier. This local law differed slightly from the early demotic law that had been introduced to the Theban region by the Saite reformers. In practice, however, both scribal and legal systems existed side by side in Thebes for decades. Since the capital Sais was hundreds of miles away in the Delta, local customs and laws could linger on for some time.

As was seen above in P. Louvre E 7861, an abnormal hieratic contract always contains an oath before Amun and Pharaoh. In this case the husband stated that unless his wife committed adultery, she would receive ample compensation in case of a divorce:

> As Amun lives, as Pharaoh lives. May he be healthy and may Amun grant him victory. If I repudiate Mrs. Tsendjehuty whose mother is Ruru, my sister who is mine, and if I am the cause for this harsh fate that will beset her, because I wish to repudiate her or because I prefer other women above her—except in the case of the large crime that is (usually) found in a woman—I will give her two deben of silver and fifty sacks (in oipe) of grain, apart from all profit and gain that I will make with her, as well as part of my own inheritance of father and mother, belonging to the children <she> has given birth to for me.

This practical attitude towards marriage, divorce, and maintenance is characteristic of legal proceedings in the Late Period. If the bride negotiated a good marriage contract, she could at least look forward to solid financial compensation. Apart from four thousand liters of grain and 182 grams of silver, in the event of divorce Mrs. Tsendjehuty would also receive part of the wealth she had acquired together with her husband, as well as part of his parental inheritance. Making a promise is of course different from keeping a promise, especially in an acrimonious divorce.

Some marriage contracts contained extremely generous settlements. One other abnormal hieratic contract dealing with a woman's marital property arrangement, P. Louvre E 7849 from 590 BCE, was found with the papers of Djekhy & Son. In that contract the bridegroom promises his bride that she will get everything in case of a divorce. It seems that even in ancient Egypt, a man could be reduced to bad decisions by a pair of beautiful eyes.

One should keep in mind, however, that contracts like P. Louvre E 7846 were an exception. Usually, if a couple wanted to establish a household, they would simply live together without putting anything in writing. This was called *hemes* (pronounced with a sharp h), or 'sitting (with someone).' These would probably still often be prearranged 'marriages.'

The true significance of documents such as P. Louvre E 7846 is reflected in the famous story of Setne and Tabubu from the Ptolemaic Period. Setne was a son of Ramesses II (reigned 1290–1224 BCE) who became a beloved folk-tale figure in the centuries after his death, embarking on all kinds of (often magical) adventures. Tabubu is what we would call a player today. Setne saw her one day on the large square before the temple and was immediately smitten by her beauty. His longing made him no match for Tabubu, who played an intricate game of cat and mouse with him:

Then Setne said to Tabubu: "Let us now crown the affair we came for."

But she answered him saying: "Then you'd better go home, where you belong. I am someone from the priestly class, I am not a humble person. If you want to do with me what you like, you must have a contract of maintenance made for me as well as a contract in which you part with all your possessions." And he said: "Well, bring in the schoolmaster, then," and he was collected immediately. He had a contract of maintenance made for her as well as a contract to part with all his possessions. At that moment someone said to Setne: "Your children are downstairs." He said: "Have them brought up." Tabubu rose and put on a veil of royal linen. Setne could see all parts of her body shining through. His lust became worse than it already was, and Setne said: "Tabubu, now let me crown the affair I came for."

But she answered him: "Then you'd better go home, where you belong. I am someone from the priestly class, I am not a humble person. If you want to do with me what you like, you must have your children countersign my contract. Make sure they will not be able to sue my children over your possessions." He had someone collect his children and made them sign the contract. Then Setne said to Tabubu: "Tabubu, now let me crown the affair I came for."

But she answered him: "Then you'd better go home, where you belong. I am someone from the priestly class, I am not a humble person. If you want to do with me what you like, you must have your children killed. Make sure they will not be able to sue my children over your possessions." And Setne said: "In that case this dreadful scheme of yours must be done to them." She had his children killed in his presence and had them thrown from the window onto the street to feed the dogs and cats. They devoured their flesh, and he could hear it happen. But he toasted with Tabubu. And Setne said to Tabubu: "Tabubu, now let me crown the affair I came for."

Only to wake up stark naked with a stiff member in a pot full of ointment. This tale is probably the first known description of a wet dream, but it also tells us about the actual value of a contract like P. Louvre E 7846. It would guarantee a woman's carefree old age, even if she never remarried.

It often happens in Egyptology that different scholars are working independently on the same subject at the same time. Thus about fifty years ago two books were published dealing with the ancient Egyptian 'marriage contracts': *Ägyptische Eheverträge* (1960) by the German demotist Erich Lüddeckens, and *Marriage and Matrimonial Property in Ancient Egypt: A Contribution to Establishing the Legal Position of the Woman* (1961) by the Dutch legal historian and demotist Pieter Willem Pestman.

What we are calling here 'marriage contracts' are not contracts of marriage per se, but arrangements dealing with the present and future possessions and daily maintenance made on the occasion of a marriage. As with ancient Egyptian land leases, we owe nearly all of our knowledge on this subject largely to the efforts of two pioneers from the 1960s.

Papyrus Louvre E 7846 was written to replace a similar contract drawn up for Mrs. Tsendjehuty and Iturech son of Petiese seven years earlier, prompting the serious question by a famous Egyptologist whether ancient Egyptian law recognized a seven-year trial period, perhaps due to a seven-year itch, long before the concept was thought to have arisen. (In Germany, for instance, the Christian Democrat politician Gabriele Pauli proposed to disband marriages automatically after seven years and to have partners renew their vows or dissolve the marriage forever.) Seven years seems quite a long time to figure out whether one wishes to keep one's wife, and there may be a more pragmatic reason for the drawing up of the new contract. Children may have been born during that time, rendering the earlier marital property arrangements obsolete.

One of the questions often asked in connection with the archive of Djekhy & Son is why it contains so many documents that seem to bear no relation to the archivists. As already discussed, a number of possible reasons come easily to mind (see above, "Between 675 and 572 BCE").

When August Eisenlohr bought the archive in Egypt there was not a single Egyptian antiquities dealer, even one as experienced as Muhammad Muhassib, with the language skills that would have enabled him to group together abnormal hieratic contracts by date and subject matter, including even related early demotic documents. There was also not a single Egyptologist who could read abnormal hieratic. The only people who could have grouped these documents together were the archivists themselves, suggesting that these seemingly unconnected texts were deposited in the archive in antiquity, even if we may not understand why.

The place of P. Louvre E 7846 in the archive of Djekhy & Son, for instance, was a mystery for many years. It is only very recently that the solution has come to light, namely the abnormal hieratic P. Louvre E 7848 from 559 BCE, written ten years before the contract renewing the marriage settlement.

In 559 BCE Djekhy had a business quarrel with his colleague Petosiris son of Iturech about the choachytes' rights to a tomb in the Theban necropolis. It is not known whether the men were related, but Djekhy was the owner of the right to service the tomb together with the children of the choachyte Teos son of Amunirtais (the father-in-law in P. Louvre E 7846). One of these children was called Khausenmut. In 536 BCE, this Khausenmut would transfer half the rights to two other tombs in the Theban necropolis to Djekhy's son Iturech (P. Louvre E 7843). In other words, these families knew each other and did business together over generations.

The choachyte Teos son of Amunirtais also had a daughter called Tsendjehuty, the 'bride' in P. Louvre E 7846. It is even possible that she was one of Djekhy's business partners in the tomb over which the quarrel had arisen in 559 BCE. In ancient Egypt—as in the modern world—people would not keep their most important documents in the home but turn them over to a trustee. For Tsendjehuty, that document was the contract that gave her financial rights in her home, and who could have been a better trustee than her 'uncle' Djekhy, a reliable business associate of her family since her early youth? Alternatively, it is possible that Djekhy had retired or died by 549 BCE, and that it was in fact his son Iturech who became the keeper of P. Louvre E 7846. *Si non è vero è ben trovato.*

Papyrus Insinger: A Saite Wisdom Text?

Papyrus Insinger is an important pedagogical wisdom text named after its first Dutch owner, Jan Herman Insinger, who bought the text from the

French antiquities dealer Frenay in Akhmim. This was still the age of the colorful antiquities hunters, and Frenay clearly had good contacts. When Wallace Budge of the British Museum spoke to him in 1887, Frenay even told him that it was he who had sold to Gaston Maspero, the director of the Service d'Antiquités Égyptiennes, all the Coptic papyri and manuscripts recently bought by the Louvre—a story that does not reflect well on Maspero, which of course may have been Frenay's intention.

Whether this is evil gossip or plain truth will be for historians to decide, although it seems that Frenay had much to gain by spreading false rumors about his competitors. When the collector Charles Wilbour visited him, for instance, Frenay told him that the infamous antiquities hunter Amélineau had tried to break into the White Monastery of Sohag to steal valuable manuscripts. Legend has it that he drugged some of the monks during their watch. The White Monastery had gained renown under the leadership of the famed Saint Shenuda, and by the fifth century CE it housed approximately 2,200 monks and 1,800 nuns. Its library was unique, and in the end Frenay himself managed to buy its manuscripts on behalf of the French Bibliothèque Nationale.

Jan Herman Insinger had moved to Egypt in 1878. He suffered from tuberculosis and expected the Egyptian climate would improve his health. He stayed in Egypt until his death in 1918, acquiring many antiquities for the Rijksmuseum van Oudheden in Leiden. P. Insinger is one of the most important of the pieces he acquired.

The papyrus, measuring over six meters, dates to the last Ptolemaic pharaohs and maybe even slightly later. Fragments of copies are known from papyrus collections in Philadelphia, Copenhagen, Florence, Cairo, Paris, and Heidelberg, to name just a few. So, like the wisdom text of Ankhsheshonqy (discussed in more detail below), the text inscribed on P. Insinger was kept and read in multiple places.

Demotists still disagree about its origin. Some say the maxims of P. Insinger stem from the time the text was written. Others believe that specific graphical elements and the language used point to an origin dating as far back as the early Saite Period—around the time the choachyte Djekhy was working in Thebes to establish the business that would become Djekhy & Son.

The content sometimes shows remarkable parallels to a Jewish manuscript known as The Wisdom of Jesus, Son of Sirach (Ecclesiasticus), a text that forms part of the so-called Septuagint—the translation of the seventy men—referring to the Greek translation of the Old Testament made before the turn of the millennium. The Septuagint is part of the biblical canon of the Catholic Church and some Orthodox Christian branches, but is not recognized by Protestants. An echo of this Jesus Ben Sirach is sometimes faintly reflected in the Jewish Talmud. The name Ecclesiasticus is an abbreviation of *liber ecclesiasticus*—Latin for 'church book'—derived from the Latin church fathers.

For our purpose, which is to penetrate some of the norms and values of the ancient Egyptians, none of this is hugely relevant. Whether or not it was influenced by the Hellenistic and Jewish tradition, P. Insinger remains a genuinely Egyptian source. It may even have been written down in an attempt to preserve a national heritage in an increasingly multicultural world. Some of the commentary in P. Insinger on relations between men and women transcends time:

> *P. Insinger col. III 16:*
> Don't be with a woman who has been with a man higher in rank than you.
> *col. VI 20:*
> (The man) who is cheeky with other men will be popular with women.

Hidden, but doubtless valuable, gems of advice in a text that addresses countless subjects besides women. The wisdom text of Ankhsheshonqy, in contrast, is much more single-minded in its focus on women in ancient Egypt.

The Teachings of Ankhsheshonqy

Like P. Insinger, the teachings of Ankhsheshonqy form a collection of maxims and admonitions. This text, now kept in London as P. BM EA 10508, was written in Akhmim during the second half of the Ptolemaic Period. Parallel texts and fragments can be found in Paris (P. Louvre N 2414 and 2377, P. Sorbonne 1260), Cairo (P. Caïro CG 30682), and Copenhagen (P. Carlsberg 304).

The teachings of Ankhsheshonqy may have been written in the Ptolemaic Period, but the thoughts behind it are much older. The original text probably dates back to the sixth or fifth century BCE, which would make it roughly contemporary to the maxims of Confucius. It was properly published for the first time in 1955 by the British Egyptologist Stephen

Glanville as *The Instructions of Onchsheshonqy*. Together with the much later *Die Lehre des Anchscheschonqi* (1991) by the German demotist Heinz-Josef Thissen, this text can now be said to be fully published.

In 2007, a new translation was published incorporating the latest insights by two German demotists, Friedhelm Hoffmann and Joachim Quack, in their *Anthologie der demotischen Literatur*. Ankhsheshonqy's collection of maxims and admonitions is embedded into a frame narrative, telling how he unwillingly became witness to a murder plot and as a result was thrown in prison for the rest of his life. The authorities did allow him to teach his son from prison, but refused to supply papyrus. All his wisdom was therefore written on ostraca, which helps to explain why the teachings are not in systematic order. Life in prison clearly gave Ankhsheshonqy a great deal of time to think about women, as it still does today:

Ankhsheshonqy col. 8, x + 12:
Do not start a relationship with a woman whose husband is still alive, so that he will not become your enemy.
col. 8, x + 22:
A wise woman is the blessing for possessions.
col. 9, x + 12:
Do not live in one house with your parents-in-law.
col. 11, x + 7:
Marry if you're twenty, so that you will have a son while you're still young.
col. 12, x + 13–14:
Show your wife your wealth, but do not entrust it to her, neither should you entrust her yearly allowance to her (all at once).
col. 13, x + 12:
If you find your wife with her lover, find yourself a better bride.
col. 13, x + 16:
Do not open your heart to your wife. Anything you tell her will end up on the street.
col. 14, x + 15:
Let no woman in your house not be pregnant or not give birth to children.
col. 15, x + 15:
Do not allow your son to choose a wife from somewhere else, so that he will not be taken from you.

col. 18, x + 9:

Give a wise woman a hundred pieces of silver, but do not take two hundred from a stupid woman.

col. 18, x + 15:

Do not rejoice too much over the beauty of your wife. What she wants is someone to sleep with her.

col. 20, x + 19:

It depends on a man's behavior whether his wife allows someone to sleep with her.

col. 20, x + 22–25:

It is a waste to have a house and not live in it. It is a waste to have a wife and not know (i.e., have sex with) her. It is a waste of a donkey to carry bricks. It is a waste of a ship to carry straw.

col. 21, x + 14:

He who is ashamed to sleep with his wife will not have children.

col. 21, x + 18–19:

Do not sleep with a woman who has a husband. He who sleeps in a bed with a married woman, his wife will be slept with on the floor.

col. 22, x + 6–8:

He who loves a street tramp, his purse will be slit open on the side. One does not load beams on a donkey. If a woman loves a crocodile, she will assume his behavior.

col. 23, x + 6–7:

Do not love a woman who has a husband. He who loves a woman who has a husband will be killed on the threshold.

col. 24, x + 10:

A man screws even better than a donkey. His only limitation is his purse.

col. 24, x + 21:

A beautiful woman with a noble character is like food in times of hunger.

col. 25, 8 + 8:

Do not bother with women's talk.

col. 25, x + 15:

Choose a wise man for your daughter, not a rich man.

col. 25, x + 17–22:

Do not marry a godless woman, so that she will not give your children a godless upbringing. If a woman lives in peace with her husband, he will never fare badly. If a woman is babbling behind the back of her husband, he certainly will not fare well. If a woman does not look after the possessions of her husband, she has an eye for another man. A slutty woman has a short life. A bad woman has no husband.

Much of what Ankhsheshonqy wrote still sounds familiar today, suggesting that his rather ambivalent view on women seems rooted in life experience.

The written evidence on the position of Egyptian women in the Late Period is conflicting. A passage from P. Mattha on the division of the inheritance of a man who dies without a will (quoted below in "Iturech Buys a Son") clearly shows that male children were rated higher than female children. It is probably also not a coincidence that the women in the archive of Djekhy & Son remain mere names.

On the other hand, there are scores of examples of ancient Egyptian women who became very successful in their own businesses, including Hatshepsut who became pharaoh. These women concluded their own contracts, like the women who made up 25 percent of the house owners in the Theban neighborhood called The House of the Cow (see above, "The Family"). Herodotus wrote that the customs and laws of the Egyptians were for the most part contrary to those of all other men, because the women went out to buy and sell, whereas the men stayed at home to weave textiles (II 35). To a Greek traveling in Egypt in the fifth century BCE, the power of Egyptian women was apparently some cause for concern.

Similar inconsistencies can be seen in ancient Egyptian women's status within the marriage. In P. Louvre E 7846, the marital property arrangement is effectively a deal between father-in-law and son-in-law about a woman referred to as "my sister, who is mine." In contrast, Diodorus Siculus, who lived several centuries later, stated that the Egyptian women were the sole authority in the household, because according to the standard Egyptian marriage contract the men had to always obey their wives. It is not hard to see how a marital property arrangement like that in P. Louvre E 7846 could be a powerful tool in the hands of a woman looking for trouble. Judging by the passage from the story of Setne and Tabubu, the ancient Egyptians themselves did see the potential drawbacks of these arrangements, even if their ultimate aim was to ensure that a woman was taken care of in case of death or divorce.

The status of ancient Egyptian women may have changed to some extent after the conquest of Egypt by Alexander the Great, when the country came under Hellenistic influence. In a number of bilingual family archives written in Greek and demotic we can actually see the mechanism of both Greek and local law at work. The famous archive of a priest of Hathor called Totoes from the second century BCE was found intact in what may have been his own house near the temple of Hathor at Deir al-Medina. The archive was locked in two sealed jars. The main character in Totoes' archive, however, is his wife Tatehathyris, who is seen acting on her own in the demotic contracts, but is represented by a legal guardian—alternately her brother Pikos and her husband Totoes—in the Greek documents.

When Tatehathyris's father died around 110 BCE she inherited a small field called The Tip. Like Iturech, the second known owner of the archive of Djekhy & Son, she leased this field to others for the duration of one year. Between 110 and 100 BCE, five lease contracts were written for this field. In two of these (written in Ptolemaic demotic), Tatehathyris is named as the actual lessor; in the other three (written in Greek), her husband Totoes states that he is the owner of this field, even though we know this was not the case. These intriguing documents show how on the microscale of the ancient Egyptian workfloor things were imperceptibly yet constantly changing. In this particular case the change may have been due to the increasing influence of Hellenistic law.

This appears to have been a setback for ancient Egyptian women, though one that is hardly confined to that time or place. As recently as 1956, a married Dutch woman was not allowed to conclude legal contracts herself. She could not even have work done in the garden by a professional gardener without her husband's permission. Dutch working women who married were automatically expected to resign from their jobs. In 1956 Dutch women were still seen first and foremost as the mothers of their children—twenty-five centuries after Djekhy & Son had stopped doing business.

4

Water
Djekhy 559 BCE

A Hostile Takeover

27 September 559 BCE (Papyrus Louvre E 7848)

The ancient Egyptians were not so very different from us. Most could probably not be bothered about great cultural achievements like the pyramids, the Book of the Dead, and other elevated theological concepts. These would always remain the domain of a small elite. The lives of ancient Egyptians were certainly no easier than the lives of people today. They did have a much shorter life expectancy, but this is a relatively recent difference: even in the Netherlands, life expectancy did not exceed forty years as recently as 1850.

One suspects that Djekhy's response would have been quite predictable when he heard that the choachyte Petosiris son of Iturech was spreading the news that he had acquired the rights to service the mummies in a rock tomb in the Theban necropolis. For a choachyte, whose income depended on supplying professional services to sustain the afterlife of the deceased, a new tomb—sometimes containing scores of mummies—meant new income. If all went well, the services rendered by a choachyte could evolve into a long-term business relationship with paying customers.

This alleged new contract to service the tombs also involved a man called Ankhhor son of Iturech, but we know nothing about his relationship to Petosiris. It is possible, since they were both sons of a man called Iturech, that Petosiris and Ankhhor were brothers. Iturech was, however, a very common name in Saite Thebes, so no definite conclusions can be drawn. Business relationships like that described by P. Louvre E 7848 often involved a variety of blood ties of which we know nothing.

The new 'owner' of the rights to service the mummies in the tomb may well have been Djekhy's cousin. But where did these choachytes come from?

A Five-thousand-year Tradition

The choachyte ('water-pourer') Djekhy son of Tesmontu was part of an ancient Egyptian tradition. The importance of water in Egypt was well known. A low Nile meant starvation. When Djekhy brought his libations—and no doubt beer, bread, and other foodstuffs as well—to the dead in the Theban necropolis this tradition had already spanned thousands of years. In Naqada in the south of Egypt, for instance, already in prehistoric times the dead were provided with all kinds of things useful for the afterlife. Offerings to the dead were primarily the responsibility of the direct family, but it is likely that a system soon developed whereby the authorities assigned specific caretakers to the funerary cults of favorite courtiers and high officials, or people even decided to go into the funerary business themselves.

Water was essential in these funerary cults. In the Old Kingdom (2575–2134 BCE) people passing the tombs in the necropolis were called upon by the deceased themselves: "You, who are still living on earth and are passing this grave, pour some water for me!"

It sounds like a lamentation betraying centuries of experience, in a country where the desert is always near. We ourselves will probably tend to the graves of our parents during our lifetime, but by the time our children have grown up these same graves will have become an abstraction that needs no further maintenance. This is probably what happened with ancient Egyptian funerary offerings: they would have been provided by the children of the deceased, and perhaps their children after them, but from then on the dead—unless they were part of some state cult or were looked after by servants paid by a rich family—would have to rely on the goodwill of accidental passersby.

Thousands of years after the Old Kingdom complaint was recorded, this sentiment was still very much alive. It appeared, for instance, in the necropolis of Akhmim. In the demotic text on a stela that is now in Chicago under inventory number 31673, the scribe Inaros son of Petemin begs any passersby to give him water. The text was published by the Egyptian demotist Adel Farid in a book with a title of heartwarming nineteenth-century length, *Fünf demotische Stelen aus Berlin, Chicago, Durham,*

*London und Oxford mit zwei demotischen Türinschriften aus Paris und einer
Bibliographie der demotischen Inschriften* (1995):

> Recitation by the scribe of the Domain of Min, the Osiris (deceased)
> Inaros son of Petemin, born from Taseba. I have spent seventy years on
> earth up to regnal year 2, third month of the akhet season, day 29, the
> day I went to my fathers. . . . I spent year after year being responsible
> for the measuring of the wine slopes in the district of Akhmim. . . . Any
> person on earth who reads this inscription, may he pour water for me.

The Egyptians also talked to their dead relatives. On a clay pot from
Qaw, a man called Shepsy—clearly in a conflict with a man called Mr.
Sobekhotep—addresses his deceased mother. The pot was found in situ in
1924 in tomb 7695 in Qaw al-Kabir. It is dated to somewhere between the
Sixth and Eleventh Dynasties. The text was published by Alan Gardiner
and Kurt Sethe—both prominent Egyptologists—in *Egyptian Letters to
the Dead Mainly from the Old and Middle Kingdoms* (1928). Shepsy's address
is actually directed to his father and mother. It is full of reproach, showing not only that the living felt a strong bond with the dead, but also
that they were well aware that they were managing the eternal life of the
deceased. In any case Shepsy did not feel any qualms about telling off his
own deceased mother:

> So I am being shortchanged here before you, the children being
> dissatisfied with me, their father? Then who will be pouring water for
> you? Would that you judge between me and Sobekhotep!

The implication is clear. It was wise for a deceased Egyptian to have
his or her water management in place. Blind faith in friendly passersby
or demanding sons had its disadvantages. That is why, in the course of
Egyptian history, the market introduced itself here, culminating in a professional branch of water-pourers for the dead, whose only concern was
to bring offerings to the deceased. For a fee, of course.

Some Egyptologists who have studied the ancient Egyptian economy
seem to deny the existence of a market of demand and supply. Instead,
they view the Egyptian economy as a system based on reciprocity and
redistribution, also known as the 'palace economy.' The British Egyptologist Chris Eyre, however, probably summarized this rather tedious

discussion correctly: "The market is detectable, if only it is looked for." It might be more accurate to say that the ancient Egyptian economy was a market system never encountered before or since. We know for instance that there was a physical market on the bank of the Nile, where manufacturers, (state) agents, and salespersons exchanged their goods, all expecting to make a profit. Looking for a profit is part of the human condition. Djekhy & Son were no exception.

Naturally, not everybody could afford the services of a professional choachyte, so in most cases the offerings to the dead remained the responsibility of the family. We know this from the written sources found in and around Deir al-Medina, the Montaillou of ancient Egypt. The rite of pouring water for the dead continued to be practiced for thousands of years. In 1916 the British Egyptologist Aylward Blackman was traveling through Nubia. There he witnessed an old woman who each Friday brought her weekly libation, a fact that reminded him strongly of the rite performed by Djekhy & Son in the Theban necropolis in 550 BCE:

> At the head of the grave there is a handmade polished red bowl to receive the libation offering. In Derr, where I saw this rite being performed more than once, the woman not only filled the bowl with water, but also sprinkled the grave itself, while saying prayers in Nubian, or just some pious wishes. (*Journal of Egyptian Archaeology* 3 [1916])

In a much more recent publication, the French Egyptologist Claude Traunecker wrote that this rite is still being performed today in the villages surrounding Esna in the south of Egypt. Chances are that the ancient pagan libation rite is still very much alive in many more villages in Egypt. Djekhy & Son are therefore part of a long tradition. However, the phrase used to denote their profession—*wah mu*, meaning both 'pouring water' and 'water-pourer'—was so far as we know only used from the New Kingdom (1550–1070 BCE) onward.

In the Old Kingdom, funerary services for the (well-off) deceased were provided by people called the *hemu ka*, literally 'the servants of the ka.' The ka was the 'double' of the living man or woman, fashioned by the god Khnum of Elephantine on a potter's wheel together with the person. This ka is often associated with what we would call the soul. In a society in which life after death was important—much more so than in many places today—the servants of the ka guaranteed immortality. According to tradition the eldest son was responsible for the mortuary cult of his parents and forefathers, though he was no more immune to distraction than his modern counterpart.

For an improved focus on this rite we will have to turn to the village of Deir al-Medina in the New Kingdom. This gated workers' community was the home of the men—and their families—who cut out the rock tombs in the Valley of the Kings, decorating them with ritual scenes and inscriptions. These were privileged men receiving good wages. They were in fact pampered by the Egyptian authorities, because they knew state secrets, such as where exactly the pharaohs had been buried and how to get there unseen. The monthly salary of an ordinary workman amounted to more than four hundred liters of grain per month, which was more than enough to sustain a family. In addition, they also received other rations, like beer, bread, cakes, fish, and wood. Those who could moonlighted on the side by manufacturing royal quality statuettes for private buyers.

These men knew what they were worth. The strikes from the twenty-ninth regnal year of Ramesses III (reigned 1194–1163 BCE) have become infamous in this respect. In that year the wages—as usual paid in kind—were increasingly often late. One surmises that the lavish donations made by Ramesses III to the temples, as documented in P. Harris I (see below, "Papyrus Rylands 9"), had done their share to drain the state's resources. From time to time the entire crew of workmen would leave Deir al-Medina and stage a sit-in at one of the royal funerary temples on the west bank of the Nile, just to put pressure on the authorities. Contemporary reports to these authorities were quite frank, as we can see from a famous memo addressed to Ta, the vizier of Ramesses III, which is also an excellent example of the way an official letter was written in ancient Egypt:

> To the fan-bearer on Pharaoh's right side, the overseer of the city and vizier Ta. The scribe Neferhotep sends a message to his lord: in life, prosperity, health. This is a letter to let my lord know. Another message for my lord: I say to Amun-Ra King of Gods, Mut, Khonsu, to Prahorakhty, to Amun of Menset (the funerary temple of Queen Ahmose Nefertari), to Nefertari of Menset, to Amun of the Thrones of the Two Lands, to Amun of the Beautiful Encounter, to Ptah of Ramesse-Meramun, to Ptah of the Place of Beauty to the south of the

village, to Hathor Mistress of the West to its north, and to Amenophis living in the middle of the Western Side: "Keep Pharaoh l.p.h. whole, my good lord, in health. Let him celebrate millions of jubilee festivals as great ruler of all countries, for ever and ever, you being in his favor every day." Another message for my lord: "I am working on the tombs of the princes commissioned by my lord. I am working very hard in a highly praiseworthy manner. In no way am I negligent." Another message for my lord: "We have become truly impoverished here. One has allowed that all our stores coming from the treasury, granary, and storehouse have become depleted. And all this at a time the weight of a *den* stone is not light. Six oipe of grain have been taken from us and given back to us as six oipe of dirt. Let our lord take care of our main-tenance. We are indeed already dying. We are no longer alive. It is no longer given to us in any form."

Together, the six oipe of grain that had been delivered in the form of worthless chaff and dirt weighed about 120 kilograms. One takes it that this was per workman, so that the actual amount missing—slightly under 30 percent of the monthly salary—would have been considerable. The wages of the individual workmen amounted to about five thousand liters of grain per year, so that with a crew of sixty men, this village alone could count on an annual income of at least three hundred thousand liters of grain. They were privileged indeed.

The scribe of this letter—O. Oriental Institute Chicago 16991—remained polite, but had cleverly reported directly to the vizier, a ruler second only to the king. Did it have any effect? More than once the authorities were able to entice the workmen to resume their work, but the grain deliveries continued to be late, so the conflict flared up time and again. The vizier did sometimes make an effort to alleviate the situation, as is recorded in the famous Turin Strike Papyrus (P. Turin 1880), dealing with the events in year 29:

> The vizier Ta went to the north after he had arrived to take the gods of the southern region to the jubilee festival (the upcoming celebra-tion of the thirty-year reign). The chief of police Nebsemen son of Panehsy came over to say to the three foremen and the crew who were standing at the gatehouse of The Tomb (i.e., the administra-tive organization covering both Deir al-Medina and the surrounding

valleys): "The vizier has said: 'Did I not come to you for no reason at all? It was not because there was nothing to bring to you that I did not come. As for your statement "Do not take away our rations," have I been promoted to vizier to take (rations) away? Perhaps I will not give to you what someone in my position should have achieved, but there is nothing left in the granaries. However, I shall give to you what I have found there.'" The scribe of The Tomb Hori said to them: "To you will be given a half ration and I will distribute it to you in person."

Again, only a half ration. The Turin Strike Papyrus is a report on the events during the strikes in and around the village. It was submitted by the scribe Amunnakhte, who was part of the management team of Deir al-Medina. It tells us how in the end some of the workmen became so frustrated with their superiors that the situation got completely out of hand. One should, however, keep in mind that part of Amunnakhte's motivation in writing this report was to present his own role in the events in regnal year 29 in the best possible light. Maybe he was just covering his official back:

Regnal year 29, third month of the peret season. The workforce (from Deir al-Medina) passed the guard stations. They sat down in the necropolis. The three foremen went away to fetch them. Work-man Mose son of Anakhte said: "As Amun endures and the Ruler l.p.h. endures, whose wrath is worse than death. If they will take me back away from here, I will only go to bed after I have devised a plan to rob a tomb. If I don't abide by this oath, I may be punished on the spot where I took an oath in the name of Pharaoh l.p.h."

We do not know whether this resulted in trouble for Mose, but if part of Amunnakhte's aim was to besmirch the reputation of some of the inhabitants of Deir al-Medina, he probably succeeded in doing so. It seems the unfavorable economic situation during the final years of the reign of Ramesses III had spurred some villagers to take matters into their own hands and to look for additional income. The Turin Strike Papyrus meticulously records some of the crimes committed (although, as suggested above, one should be cautious in light of the possible underlying motives of the scribe):

Statement by the workman Penanuqis to the scribe Amunnakhte and the foreman Khonsu: "You are my superiors and the managers of The Tomb. Pharaoh, my good lord, has made me swear an oath of loyalty, saying: 'I will not hear a thing or see any damage in the great and deep places and still hide it.' Weserhat and Pentaweret stripped stones from the shaft of the tomb of Osiris King Ramesses II, the great god. He also took an ox branded with the mark of the (mortuary) temple of Ramesses II, which is now in his stable. Then he had sex with three married women. There was Mrs. Menat who was living with Qenna, Mrs. Tayunes who was living with Nakhtamun, and Mrs. Tawerethetepty who was living with Pentaweret. You are aware of the views of Vizier Hori when it comes to taking away stones, when it was reported to him: 'The foreman Paneb, my father, did such a thing.' Now Qenna son of Ruta has done the exact same thing at the top of the shaft of the tomb of the royal children of Osiris King Ramesses II, the great god. Show me what you will do to them or I will report them to Pharaoh, my lord, as well as to the vizier, my superior." He also stated: "Weserhat did make plans to rob his tomb and actually carried them out in the Valley of the Queens."

For us it is a good thing that some of the people in the village could read and write, and that there were scores of scribes stationed in Deir al-Medina keeping meticulous records of their activities for centuries on end. They have left us with thousands of letters, legal protocols, grocery lists, sales contracts, absence lists, and so on. A good outline of the richness of these textual sources is *Village Life in Ancient Egypt: Laundry Lists and Love Letters* by the American Egyptologist Andrea McDowell (1999), containing translations of over two hundred different (types of) texts. In Egyptology the study of this 45-by-120 meter gated community had long been neglected, but this has changed in the past thirty years, leading to a steady stream of books about the village.

As far as choachytes and funerary libations are concerned, the sources from Deir al-Medina are patchy. They tell us, for instance, that the mortuary cults of Thutmosis IV (reigned 1401–1391 BCE) and Ramesses IV (reigned 1163–1156 BCE) included professional choachytes. Even the scribe Amunhotep son of Hapu—later to be deified and one day to become the patron saint of the choachytes' association of which Djekhy and Iturech were members—had his own choachytes, as did a high priest of Amun. Other sources from the same period, however, tell us that these same choachytes could also be designated by completely different titles. Two of them, Ahauty and Pentahutnakhte, are sometimes referred to as carpenters. The choachyte Kerbaal—the name suggests an origin in Palestine—is called a slave and baker in one source and slave and choachyte in another. These shifting titles suggest that choachytes could be assigned to someone's funerary cult without payment. On the other hand, the choachytes named above were all part of the famous tomb robbery court cases that took place at the end of the New Kingdom, during the reign of Ramesses IX (reigned 1131–1112 BCE). Obviously they had looked after not only the deceased entrusted to their care, but also their own interests. An official protocol—now kept in the British Museum as P. BM EA 10053—tells us about some of the activities of the choachyte Ahauty:

> Statement about the four boards of cedar wood of the silver bottom of king Wesermare Setepenre (Ramesses II), the great god, that the scribe Sedy gave to the citizen Mrs. Taherer, the wife of the god's father Hory: "He gave them to the carpenter Ahauty of the soul chapel of Huy (Amunhotep son of Hapu), and he made this into an inner coffin for her."

A choachyte-carpenter who receives four exquisite, royal-quality boards to turn these into a coffin, without asking his client some awkward questions? The Egyptian authorities were probably not convinced of Ahauty's innocence and would have subjected him to some brutal interrogation techniques. Nor did they feel very sorry for Kerbaal, who was also arrested and questioned. In that time and place, questioning a man meant getting the required answers at any cost. In the end it was to be Kerbaal's fate to 'go downstream,' as somewhat laconically stated by the official source. Whether this was as a prisoner on a boat to the king's residence or as a dead body flung into the Nile is unknown. But in all probability, Kerbaal's career as a choachyte was cut short at this point and never resumed.

The sources from Deir al-Medina also tell us about the official visits to the village by the authorities. The vizier regularly came to inspect the progress of the work or to select a convenient spot for another royal tomb.

Official visits served not only to inspect the work on the royal tombs, but sometimes also, as we know from various sources, the occasional funerary libation to great kings of the past. For the first time we now come across the term we know from the sixth-century BCE archive of Djekhy & Son: *wah mu*.

Alongside the professional choachytes attached to royal cults, ancient Egyptians believed that even deities like Amun-Ra King of Gods, Amun-emope, and Horus performed this rite. In the Ptolemaic Period they poured water for the dead in the Theban necropolis at the beginning of each week (an Egyptian week lasted ten days). But there were no professional choachytes in New Kingdom Deir al-Medina. It was the villagers themselves who brought libations to their deceased relatives in the tomb chapels to the west of the village.

The typical Deir al-Medina tomb consisted of a walled courtyard leading to a chapel crowned by a mud-brick pyramid. This pyramid contained a niche for a stela facing the entrance of the courtyard. Below this structure a series of chambers would be cut out into the rock. The burial chambers usually had a vaulted ceiling, showing images of the deceased engaged in everyday activities. The craftsmanship of these tombs is often stunningly good because the men who built them were also responsible for the construction and decoration of the royal tombs nearby. Much of their free time was apparently spent on furnishing their own tombs, where one day people would come to pray and offer libations.

Among the artifacts dating from the fortieth regnal year of Ramesses II (1290–1224 BCE) is a beautifully preserved working roster, O. (Ostracon) BM EA 5634, tracking the attendance of the individual workmen from Deir al-Medina in the Valley of the Kings. The scribe who kept this record meticulously noted for each individual workman when and why he had not come to work. The reasons for absence vary widely, from the sting of a scorpion to the mistress of the house having her period. According to this roster, the workman Sawadjy brought a libation to his deceased father on days 24–26 of the first month of the peret season in year 40 of Ramesses II. Perhaps his father had died only recently and Sawadjy wanted to make sure he would have enough water upon his arrival in the hereafter. On day 25 of the same month, however, the workmen Nakhtmin and Paser also decided to bring libations to the dead—Paser for his son—and did not come to work. One cannot help but wonder whether Sawadjy inspired both Nakhtmin and Paser to take a day off as well, saying that they also had to offer libations to their relatives. Or perhaps they did have a valid reason for selecting this particular day 25 to bring a water offering to a deceased loved one. Their manager would have known better what we cannot tell three thousand years on, whether these men were friends, or relatives, or had some other reasonable explanation for their combined absence that day.

Because libations to the dead formed such an integral part of everyday life, the ancient Egyptians never felt the need to describe this rite. There is a single letter from Deir al-Medina that offers more information, but as is so often the case with ancient letters, it raises more questions than answers:

> The washerman Qa brought you one big loaf. Let there now be brought to me a watersack, some ink, and some incense. And also an offering table and a garland (?). On day 18. The case is that water will be poured on day 19. (O. DeM 551)

Was the scribe referring to some of the things he needed to bring a libation to the deceased? A watersack, incense, and an offering table make perfect sense in that context, but why would he need ink, given that he had just used some to write this note?

Ultimately, the village of Deir al-Medina is not a particularly informative source on the libations to the dead. We now know that these could be performed on the first day of the week and also after the funeral. But there were probably scores of other days that were appropriate for a libation, like the birthday of the deceased, the anniversary of the day they had died, or religious festival days, such as the Festival of the Valley, which Thebans celebrated in the second month of the shemu season. Already in the Middle Kingdom (2040–1640 BCE) this was known as a Theban festival of the dead, an All Souls' Day. During this festival Amun of Karnak would join a procession visiting the gods residing on the west bank of the Nile in the Theban necropolis area, which was the perfect occasion for libating to the dead. This festival was still being celebrated centuries later, during the Saite Period.

This brings us back to 27 September 559 BCE and to Djekhy & Son, who were looking for ways to counter the hostile takeover of a tomb owned by the consortium of choachytes of which Djekhy was a member. On this day, Djekhy's mind was probably preoccupied by something other than the ancient tradition he belonged to. Apparently Petosiris had been appointed as a choachyte at 'his' tomb. We do not know if Petosiris was related to Djekhy in any way, but we may assume that this appointment led to some antagonism; as far as Djekhy was aware, he and a number of his colleagues—not Petosiris—were responsible for managing this tomb. Some of these colleagues were the children of the choachyte Teos son of Amunirtais, whom we have met before in the context of his daughter's marriage contract (P. Louvre E 7846; see above, "The Family" and "Marital Property Arrangement") and his son's business partnership with Djekhy's son Iturech (P. Louvre E 7843; see below, "New Mummies, New Opportunities"). The parties involved in the takeover of the tomb in 559 BCE were:

New, self-proclaimed owners	Rightful owners
The choachytes Petosiris son of Iturech, Petedjehuty son of Inaros, and Nesamunhotep son of Peteamunip	The children of the choachyte Teos son of Amunirtais, the choachyte Khausendjehuty son of Teos and Takheru,[1] and the choachyte Djekhy son of Tesmontu

People often think of ancient Egyptians in rather elevated terms. The pharaoh Akhnaton, for instance, is still seen by many as a great visionary, whereas in reality he was probably just an average Near Eastern tyrant who was not very keen on dissident opinions. Even he had rebellious black tribes wiped out from time to time if it suited his purpose.

From the fragments of a stela found in the Egyptian border fortress of Buhen, we learn that in his twelfth regnal year, Akhnaton was displeased when a tribe from the unknown land of Akujati infiltrated a district in Nubia (the square brackets and ellipsis [. . .] indicate a lacuna in the original text):

His Majesty was in [Akhet-Aton (Amarna), and people came to tell him, saying]: "The enemies from the foreign land of Akujati, [they] are considering an uprising against Egypt, because they are coming down to [the land of] Nubia to rob it of its subsistence, while passing through [all districts]." Then His Majesty gave order to the King's Son of [Kush and Overseer of the Southern Foreign Lands (the viceroy) to mobilize an army and to strike down] the enemies of the foreign land of Akujati, me[n and women]. (. . .) List of [the booty that His Majesty received from the foreign land] of Akujati: Nubians alive 84, [. . .] together—145 persons alive. Put on the stake [. . .] together 225, makes 361.

Although this looks more like policing than full-scale war, finding yourself in Akujati at that precise moment was probably not a healthy prospect. Yet despite this, Akhnaton retains the image of being the first convinced pacifist in human history, limply lying on his couch while composing poems for his god Aton.

The point to be drawn from this is that the ancient Egyptians—it is so easily forgotten—were ordinary people just like us, with the same talents, short tempers, and worries. Theban choachytes like Djekhy would certainly have had some dirty business tricks up their sleeve. Petosiris and Djekhy were members of the same Theban choachytes' association, so before long this business quarrel would have become the talk of the town. In any case, the choachytes' rights to a tomb—specifically the rights to the profits from the tomb—were not inalienable. They could be inherited, sold, or serve as security for a loan. It is possible that the 'new' owner Petosiris believed that he did have a bona fide claim on this tomb, perhaps through inheritance. Whatever Petosiris may have believed, it is clear from the archival evidence that Djekhy felt his rights had been usurped.

Together with the other co-owners, Djekhy filed a complaint. This was probably not done at a civilian or religious court of law. The Theban choachytes' association was a highly organized network that would have had its own Articles of Association and Rules of Procedure. Many of these have come down to us from the Ptolemaic Period (332–30 BCE). They were designed to deal with every conceivable situation. A business conflict about a tomb would thus probably have been dealt with behind the closed doors of the association itself. We do not know whether the Theban choachytes had their own headquarters, but if they did it was probably located somewhere near or even in a sanctuary of Amunhotep son of Hapu, which could very well have been in the large temple compound of Amun on the east bank of the Nile.

The dispute was ultimately settled by contract—P. Louvre E 7848—through the offices of Petehorresne son of Peteamunip, the overseer of the necropolis and a man whom Djekhy knew well.[2] Djekhy had been involved in a similar conflict nine years earlier (P. Louvre E 7861), and on 29 October 552 BCE Petehorresne wrote out a receipt for him (P. Louvre E 7847), probably to settle yet another business quarrel. The declaration that ended the affair of the tomb takeover was recorded by Petehorresne as follows:

> We (the claimants) have ensured that the choachyte Petosiris son of Iturech will take an oath for us in the presence of Khonsuemwasnefer-hotep in regnal year 12, on day 13 of the second month of the shemu season, on the fifteenth day of the first month of the shemu season, stating: "The place of the mountain (the tomb) of which I have said: 'I have (. . .) received (. . .) Ankhhor son of Iturech,'—you are its choachytes, bonded with these Great Ones (the mummies in the tomb)." If he shies away from (this statement), he will take an oath for us, saying: "I have no longer any authority over it from today onward. There is no one with us: brother, sister, master, mistress, or anyone else who will be able to approach you about this matter, unto eternity."

Exit Petosiris.

It is an entirely clear statement, but there is something strange about the dating. P. Louvre E 7848 was written on 27 September 559 BCE (day 21 of the first month of the shemu season in regnal year 12 of Amasis). According to the statement above, Petosiris was to take the oath that relinquished his alleged rights to the tomb on 19 October 559 BCE, about three weeks later (day 13 of the second month of shemu in the same year 12). So why would the scribe have to mention yet another date, day 15 of the first month of shemu? Scholars were at a loss for years.

In fact the answer lies in the mention of the god Khonsuemwasnefer-hotep. Recall that this was the god before whom Djekhy swore an oath in P. Louvre E 7861 (568 BCE). Khonsuemwasneferhotep was not the patron saint of the Theban choachytes; P. Louvre E 7840, one of the records of the association written between 542 and 538 BCE, makes it clear that this was Amunhotep son of Hapu. But he is integral to comprehending the meaning of the second date, which was finally worked out by the American Egyptologist Richard Parker. His solution was as simple as it was brilliant: day 13 of the second month of the shemu season in regnal year 12 of Amasis referred to the civil calendar, whereas day 15 of the first month of the shemu season was actually a day of the lunar calendar. The full moon on day 15 of the first month of the shemu season meant that the power of Khonsuemwasneferhotep—a lunar god—would be at its height. This might discourage Petosiris from making a false oath.

P. Louvre E 7840 also mentions this fifteenth day of the first month, and by coincidence this reference is to the first month of the shemu season as well. A specific sum of money was reserved for that day, perhaps to pay the scribe who had to write a similar contract following yet another business quarrel.

P. Louvre E 7848 was found with the papers of Djekhy & Son. It is—as so often in these cases—a carefully written document betraying the effort by its scribe. No witnesses signed it. The number of witnesses to a contract of that time did vary, but it is strange to have no witnesses at all. Nonetheless, the fact that Djekhy kept P. Louvre E 7848 in his archive suggests that it gave him certain rights. The title deed to the rock tomb at the heart of the quarrel is missing, but Djekhy was only a co-owner of the tomb; the title deed may have been kept in the archive of one of his colleagues. It is also possible that Djekhy and Iturech only had the rights to service the mummies in the tomb and that the tomb itself was owned by someone else. It was common practice, during the Saite and Ptolemaic periods, to store as many mummies in a reused tomb as possible. As a result, multiple choachytes, even from competing firms, could be working in the same tomb. Finally, it is possible that P. Louvre E 7848 was merely a very carefully written draft or a copy. The issue of tomb rights is complex and requires further research, as evidenced by the passage below from P. Mattha (col. IX 30–32), the legal manual from around 250 BCE discussed above. It deals with the selling and buying of tombs, but so far no demotist or Egyptologist (including this author) has commented on the scope of its content:

> There are places made of natural stone or bricks in which to bury people. If nobody is buried there, the owner is at liberty to sell them to someone else. If people are buried there, the owner does not have the right to sell them.

Even if the tombs could not be sold, the rights to service the mummies inside the tombs certainly could (for example, P. Louvre E 7843).

It is clear from the archival material that this conflict over the rights to the tomb did not preclude further business dealings between Djekhy and his legal adversaries in the case: Petosiris, Petedjehuty son of Inaros, and Nesamunhotep son of Peteamunip. This would in any case have been difficult, given the close-knit nature of the Theban choachytes' community.

Petosiris and Djekhy collaborated just three years after their conflict over the tomb rights was resolved, when they along with thirteen others leased some twenty-five hectares of land (P. BM EA 10432, 556 BCE). Petosiris appears in the archive for the last time in 542 BCE, in the records of the Theban choachytes' association (P. Louvre 7840 II 4, III 12, and IV 21). From then on any trace of him vanishes.[3]

Meanwhile, Petedjehuty son of Inaros reappears in 547 BCE, in a business conflict with Djekhy's brother Rery (P. Cairo CG 30657). And in 555 BCE Nesamunhotep son of Peteamunip, also a choachyte, leased some fields from the Domain of Amun in partnership with Djekhy. The lease contract is now kept in Paris (P. Louvre E 7844).

It remains unclear whether these later transactions between Djekhy and his legal opponents of 559 BCE were private enterprises or agreements they concluded on behalf of the choachytes' association. Whatever the reason, the bottom line was that Djekhy was a businessman. He had avoided a hostile takeover. Now it was back to business as usual.

5

Flax
Djekhy 556–552 BCE

Working the Land

December 556–January 555 BCE (Papyrus BM EA 10432)

The office of the priest of Amun-Ra King of Gods, Psamtik son of Ankh-pakhrat became very crowded one day in the winter of 556–555 BCE, between 5 December and 4 January to be precise. This office was probably hidden somewhere in the vast compound of Amun in Karnak. The weather was cool, twenty degrees Celsius perhaps. Psamtik stood face-to-face with no fewer than fifteen men, all wanting to lease the same flax fields. Some may have been accompanied by their eldest sons (who would one day run the family business). This was probably not the only field that would have to be processed today. There were more appointments on this day, all waiting for Psamtik. And this field was no ordinary field, as we will see.

Why did the ancient Egyptians conclude a land lease? It is reasonable to assume that profits, blood ties, friendship, networking, and mutual trust were as important in the Saite Period as they are today. Maybe there was a public tender, or maybe the deal was settled privately over a good glass of wine. These are details we do not know. What we do know is that the Egyptians in the archive of Djekhy & Son liked to do business together, for instance collaborating to till someone else's land for one year. If the harvest was good, all stakeholders stood to benefit. The men who formed these business partnerships called each other *kheber*, '(business) friend.' Nearly the same word is still used in this sense in Dutch today, *gabber*, which is derived from Yiddish.

Most contracts would be concluded orally, based on the customary law. P. Mattha contains quite a few sections dealing with the leasing of land, which is to be expected in a country so dependent on agriculture (P. Mattha II 5–12). It is likely that the passages below are a reflection of the customary law that governs these leases:

> Suppose that someone tills a field and the one who tills them is in charge of them, and if the man who owns the land takes these away from him, saying: "I will not ask rental from him," and if the one who tilled the fields then files a complaint against the owner of the fields, 25 percent of the harvest from the seedcorn will be taken away from the owner of the fields and given to the one who tilled the fields as a compensation for his work.
>
> Suppose that the one who tills the fields is not in charge of them, (. . .) the one who tills them, whereas he has tilled them with seedcorn belonging to someone else, and if the owner of the fields takes the fields away from him and if the one who has tilled the fields then files a complaint against the owner of the fields, 25 percent of the harvest from the seedcorn will be taken away from the owner of the fields and given to the one who tilled the fields as compensation for his work and his seedcorn.
>
> Suppose that someone draws up a lease contract for a number of fields and the owner of the fields supplies him with seedcorn. If the one who had the lease contract drawn up does not till the fields and receives the seedcorn after the fields have been inundated and manured, he is still obliged to give the harvest from the seedcorn as described in the lease contract that he has drawn up.
>
> Suppose that someone draws up a lease contract for a number of fields and the owner of the fields supplies him with seedcorn. If then there is a year without inundation, he is not obliged to pay the lease, but he will have to return the seedcorn.

The scenarios described in P. Mattha were undoubtedly very common. But for particularly complicated agreements, written leases would be preferable. If people took the trouble to have a written lease drawn up, it was usually because there were special circumstances that made an oral agreement unsatisfactory. In the case of P. BM EA 10432, there were no fewer than fifteen lessees who all wanted to be mentioned by name, probably because each was concerned to keep an accurate record of his percentage in the lease agreement. Their eagerness in this particular case probably had something to do with the quality of the land: it was located in The Palette of Khonsu, an area that belonged to the national elite.

The papyrus on which this lease contract was written is now kept in the British Museum. The contract was written in abnormal hieratic. It has broken off at the bottom, so that the name of the scribe is lost, but it is believed to have been Peteamunip son of Petehorresne from the well-known Theban family of scribes described above (see above, "The Saite Restoration").

Although Djekhy is one of the lessees, strictly speaking this contract does not belong to the archive of Djekhy & Son because the papyrus was found—or at least offered for sale—fifty years earlier than the Eisenlohr collection. Any of the fifteen lessees could have kept the document in his archive, so it probably ended up in the archive of the first person listed, the overseer of the troop Neshorbehedety ('He belongs to Horus of Edfu'), who is otherwise unknown. It is probable that that the troop referred to here was actually the group of fifteen lessees. In true Egyptian style Neshorbehedety had also brought his son Hor into this deal.

A lease contract like this was only valid for a year. Its value would decrease after the lease had expired, although it would stand as proof that the listed tenant(s) had leased a specific plot before. Thus it could still be useful at a later date.

It is unknown whether the fifteen lessees were there in person when P. BM EA 10432 was drafted or whether they were represented by a single spokesman, a practice known from the archive of Djekhy & Son.[1] The tenants are listed in Table 4.

Most of the men listed here as Djekhy's business partners, those marked with (*), are only known from this document. Some others are only known from the records of the Theban choachytes' association (P. Louvre E 7840). But a few are choachytes who appear elsewhere in the Djekhy & Son archive and so about whom we have a bit more information. One of these is Petosiris son of Iturech, Djekhy's erstwhile legal opponent (P. Louvre E 7848; see above). Another is the choachyte Chayutayudeny son of Peteamunip, who appears in the archive a few times. This very rare name means 'They have taken their share.' In ancient Egypt names often referred to the gods; in that context, 'They have taken their share' almost sounds like a cynical reference to brothers and sisters who died before this child was born.

Table 4. Tenants in P. BM EA 10432, in order

Neshorbehedety son of Hor (*)	Overseer of the troop
Djehutyirtais son of Petehorpakhrat (*)	
Petosiris son of Iturech	Choachyte
Inaros son of Petehorresne (*)	
Chayutayudeny son of Peteamunip	Choachyte
Horkheb son of Khonsuirau (*)	
Rery son of Payuyuyu	Choachyte
Payuyuenhor son of Petedjehuty (*)	Choachyte
Ihudjehuty son of Inaros (*)	Choachyte
Djekhy son of Tesmontu	Choachyte
Hor son of Neshorbehedety (*)	
Iturech son of Paweher (*)	
Hor son of Amunirankh (*)	
Nesnebankh son of Horpaykhrat (*)	
Peteamunip son of Ituru	Choachyte

There is no direct connection between Chayutayudeny and the documents in the archive of Djekhy & Son mentioning his name and Dkekhy in a single document, except here in P. BM EA 10432. These documents may have ended up with Djekhy's papers through his role as a trustee of the Theban choachytes' association. In one, the same Chayutayudeny appears to be acting on behalf of another joint venture of choachytes (P. Louvre E 7845A). Although Djekhy is not directly named in that text, it is conceivable that he participated in the agreement it documents. Chayutayudeny is also mentioned in P. Louvre E 7845B, a very damaged contract written in the right margin of P. Louvre E 7845A, drawn up to divide a crop between Chayutayudeny and an otherwise unknown man. Much more interesting is the mention of Chayutayudeny son of Peteamunip in P. Louvre E 7128 (511 BCE), in which he is identified as an overseer of the necropolis. But this Chayutayudeny had a different mother, so it is unlikely to be the same man who entered into a land lease with Djekhy; perhaps it was his grandson? From the fact that overseers of the necropolis sometimes attended new year's meetings of the Theban choachytes' association (P. Louvre E 7840), we can infer that there were close ties between these groups; it is possible they were close enough for a choachyte to be promoted to overseer of the necropolis.

The list of lessees is the most interesting part of this contract; the remainder is something of an anticlimax. The lessees tell the landlord Psamtik:

> You have leased to us the flax fields in The Palette of Khonsu that were sown with flax from regnal year 14 to regnal year 15. We are the ones who will grow flax on them from regnal year 15 to regnal year 16. When harvest has occurred in regnal year 16 you will receive 25 percent of the flax we will produce [. . .].

And that is where the papyrus breaks off. The basic agreement is clear: the landlord will receive 25 percent of the harvest. Later land leases from the archive of Djekhy & Son show that the parties involved generally thought of everything, including the estimation of the harvest by the scribes of the temple and the payment of the harvest tax of the Domain of Amun. It may be that these details were recorded in the part of the document that has been lost, or perhaps simply that the creativity of the scribe petered out after drawing up the long list of tenants. He did not identify the neighboring plots of the flax fields that were the subject of the lease. We know only that they were located in The Palette of Khonsu, a farming area evidently known to any Theban citizen, but not to us.

The Palette of Khonsu

A slightly later land lease from the archive of Djekhy & Son, P. Louvre E 7845A (described in further detail below), does describe the boundaries of The Palette of Khonsu. It was surrounded by fields connected with the funerary cult of the vizier Pamy and fields belonging to the Adoratrice of Amun, the highest priestess of the land. Pamy had been a powerful ruler in his day. His sons Peteamaunet and Pakhar both became viziers themselves, as did Peteamaunet's son Nespakashuty. Vizier Nespakashuty and his uncle Pakhar also married daughters of Pharaoh Takelot III (seventh century BCE).

Little is known about Pamy. On a small Osiris statue in the British Museum (EA 22913) he refers to himself as "scribe of the temple in the

Domain of Amun, accountant of the Domain of Amun, overseer of the city, and vizier." Funerary objects found with his descendants also call him a "third prophet of Amun." It seems that some ancient Egyptians were as interested in collecting titles as their counterparts in modern old boys' networks.

Pamy was found buried alongside members of his closest family in a crypt in the funerary temple complex of Queen Hatshepsut in Deir al-Bahari. Parts of his coffin were found during an excavation by the Metropolitan Museum of Art (New York) in the 1930–31 season. This suggests that The Palette of Khonsu was not just a plot of arable land, but one belonging to the economic, religious, and political elite of the time. For centuries this would remain a well-known farming area in the Theban region. It is still mentioned five hundred years later in an ostracon now kept in the British Museum, O. BM EA 31681, a receipt showing that the land was used to farm grain.

The lease contracts from the Saite Period never record the size of a leased field, so we can only make an educated guess at the dimensions of the fields in The Palette of Khonsu. We can infer that it was reasonably large from the number of lessees in P. BM EA 10432. Let us assume that each of the fifteen lessees stood to receive 5 percent of the harvest, knowing that the landlord received 25 percent. Let us also assume that the land was sown with emmer instead of flax and that each of the lessees needed this 5 percent share to maintain his family. Egyptologists have calculated that an average ancient Egyptian family could live on fifty sacks (four thousand liters) of grain per year. If each 5 percent share of the field yielded fifty sacks of grain (and thus allowed the lessee to support his family), the output of the land leased out in this contract would be a thousand sacks. We do not know exactly how much the Egyptian arura—about half a soccer field—produced; estimates vary from five to twenty sacks of grain per arura. The harvest would of course partly depend on the quality of the land. All these figures come from ancient Egyptian sources, but they do not tell us whether the land in question was very fruitful land or stony ground. If, as an average, we set the output per arura at ten sacks, this would correspond to eight hundred liters of grain, and approximately 3,200 liters per hectare. By these calculations, our fifteen lessees would have been leasing a plot of a hundred aruras, fifty soccer fields, or twenty-five hectares. It is a figure to give even a modern corporate farmer pause.[2] Then again, we know that Djekhy's son Iturech possessed more than ten hectares himself.

Around the time this lease was being concluded in Thebes, elsewhere in Egypt events were unfolding that help to correct our image of Egypt as an idyllic and morally elevated pastorale. As is so often the case in Egyptology, this is due to mere coincidence, namely the finding of P. Rylands 9.

Papyrus Rylands 9

Egyptologists studying the Late Period in Egypt have long been resigned to the fact that the attention span of most people stops at Tutankhamun or Ramesses II only to pick up again at the temples from the Ptolemaic Period. This is a shame, because many important documentary sources were written in the intermediate Kushite, Saite, and Persian periods—sources that are indispensible for our knowledge of everyday life in Egypt.

One of these sources is P. Rylands 9, a twenty-five-column papyrus written in the reign of Darius I (521–486 BCE), the Persian pharaoh of Egypt. The papyrus was found together with an archive of eight other documentary papyri, P. Rylands 1–8. P. Rylands 9 is a draft, a copy, or a copy of a draft of a petition that was made by an Egyptian called Petiese. Perhaps this petition was even addressed to the Persian satrap of Egypt. The text, mostly written in early demotic, was published in 1909 in three volumes—and brilliantly at that—by Francis Llewellyn Griffith in his *Catalogue of the Demotic Papyri in the John Rylands Library Manchester: With Facsimiles and Complete Translations*. This publication by Griffith was so good that even today, a hundred years later, it remains a key source. In the meantime, however, we have learned more about the time of Darius and early demotic. Thus the definitive publication is now considered to be the equally thorough edition published in two parts by the German demotist Günter Vittmann, *Der demotische Papyrus Rylands 9* (1998). Vittmann's edition does not contain any modern photographs, and it has sadly become impossible to take any. In the 1960s or 1970s, the Egyptologist E.A.E. Reymond treated the papyrus with some type of oil in an effort to conserve it, but instead damaged it beyond recognition. The original is thus no longer of any use for scientific purposes.

What makes P. Rylands 9 so special? For one thing, it is a highly detailed petition to the government by a native Egyptian. If we are to believe the author, Petiese, in some parts of Late Period Egypt the authorities were corrupt to the core. Without a powerful protector, you were lost. P. Rylands 9 is about plunder, murder, corruption, arson, and intimidation—not by the Persian occupation force, but by Egyptian officials and the priests of Amun in the little town of al-Hiba.

At that time al-Hiba was called Tayudjy, which translated literally means 'their walls.' In the Twenty-first Dynasty, extensive fortifications had been built there. The town lies on the east bank of the Nile, about twenty miles south of the Fayum. The temple of al-Hiba was devoted to Amun-Ra Great of Roaring Lord of the Great Rock and is believed to have been instigated by Pharaoh Sheshonq I of the Twenty-second Dynasty, who reigned from approximately 945 to 924 BCE.

The author of P. Rylands 9 is called Petiese, but his petition is a frame narrative that spans a number of generations, including the reigns of Psamtik I, Psamtik II, Apries, Amasis, and Darius I. The papyrus mentions a number of people called Petiese. They were the forefathers of the author of P. Rylands 9, who lived in the reign of Darius I. This is why the author of P. Rylands 9 is usually referred to as Petiese III. This is his simplified family tree:

Family member	Reign of
Ituru	
Petiese I	Psamtik I
Wedjasematawy I	Psamtik I
Petiese II	Psamtik II/Apries
Wedjasematawy II	Apries/Amasis
Petiese III (author P. Rylands 9)	Darius I

The actual source of all trouble is Petiese I. In his petition Petiese III rather naively describes how this Petiese I provided just about any member of his family with a lucrative priestly office in the temple. He obviously had the authority to do so and used it to the full. Petiese I managed the whole of Upper Egypt on behalf of Psamtik I. He started out as an assistant, but later became the co-administrator of the southern territory together with the great harbormaster Petiese son of Ankhsheshonq, who was a viceroy of some sort. According to the petition of Petiese III, his own forefather Petiese I had recommended Sematawytefnakht, the son of this great harbormaster, to Psamtik I so that he could succeed to his father's position in year 18. This would be strange, because already in regnal year 9 of Psamtik I Sematawytefnakht—also known from a number of statues found in the Delta—was the great harbormaster who commanded the fleet that brought princess Nitocris to Thebes, where she was to become the highest priestess of Amun in the land.

During one of his tours of inspection—perhaps even in the context of the Saite Restoration described in chapter 2—Petiese I docked at al-Hiba. There he saw that the temple was in ruins. When he asked how this had come about, he was told that the temple had suffered severely from a tax imposed during the Assyrian occupation that had never been lifted by the Egyptian authorities when Egypt was liberated. Petiese I personally made sure the temple was restored to its former glory and that the economic department of the temple was put on its feet again, partly by donating a thousand aruras of arable land. He was so self-satisfied with his good deeds that he had two granite statues of himself set up in the court of the temple, as well as a commemorative stela on which he summarized all that he had done for public display. He also had a house built in the temple court and had his children and his son-in-law Horwedja appointed as priests of Amun in al-Hiba. The great harbormaster Petiese son of Ankhsheshonq, impressed with his protégé, had his own income as a priest of Amun in al-Hiba transferred to Petiese I. It must have been quite irritating to the regular priestly staff of the temple of Amun in al-Hiba to see Petiese I—under the protection of the most powerful ruler in Upper Egypt—allot al-Hiba priesthoods to his family members and thereby rob their own relatives of an income. In regnal year 31 of Psamtik I, 634 BCE, matters came to a head:

It happened in regnal year 31 in the third month of the peret season that the grain that had grown on The God's Offering of Amun of al-Hiba was being delivered. It was collected at the temple. The priests went to the temple and said: "I say, by Ra! Now he will come again and take 20 percent of The God's Offering right before our eyes, that sniveling southerner." They recruited some sinister types and said: "Come over tonight with your clubs, lie on the grain, and bury your clubs there till the morning." Now it so happened that Horwedja son of Payfchauawybastet (the son-in-law of Petiese I) had two strong sons. When morning came the priests went to the temple to divide the grain among the phyles (the rotating priestly crews). The two sons of Horwedja son of Payfchauawybastet came to the temple and said: "Let them measure out 20 percent (for us)." The young priests took their clubs from the grain, surrounded both sons, and beat them up. They fled before them (i.e., the attackers) to the holiest part of the temple, but they were still being pursued. At the entrance to the holiest place of the temple of Amun they were overtaken and were beaten to death there and thrown into a granary.

Murder in the Cathedral, many centuries earlier in Egypt. The priests of Amun in al-Hiba had no scruples when it came to murdering colleagues who wanted their share of the harvest. In the end they got away with it; after a legal procedure without any result, an uncomfortable cease-fire was concluded between the family of Petiese I and the priests of al-Hiba.

Years later things got out of hand again. In his fourth regnal year, Psamtik II (591 BCE) visited Syria and Palestine, probably to reinforce the Egyptian presence in the region. This was a region where things were always near boiling point, and now even Babylon was being threatened by the Medes. Psamtik decided to bring a delegation of priests from as many temples as possible. At that time Petiese II, grandson of Petiese I, was serving as priest of Amun in the temple of al-Hiba, collecting 20 percent of all the income from the temple. The other priests of Amun set him up nicely:

> A message was also sent to al-Hiba that a priest was to be sent with the bouquet of Amun to accompany Pharaoh into Syria. The priests met and they all said to Petiese II son of Wedjasematawy I: "It is appropriate that you accompany Pharaoh to Syria. There is nobody in this town except you who could go to Syria. Look, you're a scribe of records. There is nothing people could ask you that would not lead to a fitting answer. You are the priest of Amun. The priests of Amun and of the (other) great gods of Egypt are the ones who will accompany Pharaoh to Syria."

Naturally, the moment Petiese II was in Syria the priests of Amun transferred his rights to 20 percent of the harvest to someone else, someone more powerful than he. Petiese II attempted to have his rights restored at the royal court, but the king was ill—or at least he said he was. Petiese II then sued the new owner of his share before the vizier and a court of law, but he did not succeed in his claim. In the end, financed by his relatives, he returned to al-Hiba, where he was given a piece of well-meant and timeless advice, which provides a useful insight into sixth-century-BCE Egypt—and indeed today:

> Petiese II son of Wedjasematawy I came north and arrived at al-Hiba. The people he met all said to him: "It's no use filing a claim in a legal court. Your opponent is richer than you. Even if you have a hundred pieces of silver, he will still make sure that you lose."

While the primary purpose of P. Rylands 9 was to end the age-old conflict between the family of Petiese III and the priests of Amun in the village of al-Hiba, the text also describes the tensions between the Royal Domain and the Domain of Amun.

All the agricultural activities by Djekhy & Son were undertaken in the Domain of Amun in Thebes. As in al-Hiba, the economic department of this domain—staffed by the priests of Amun—was called The God's Offering of Amun. P. Rylands 9 shows that its employees were not necessarily reliable. However, there is nothing in the papers left by Djekhy & Son suggesting that things were as bad in Thebes as they were in al-Hiba. But even the Domain of Amun had to compete with other entities: the other gods had their own domains, as did the political elite (and their funerary cults), and kings and their relatives.

The conflict between the Royal Domain and the Domain of Amun described in P. Rylands came to a head in the fifteenth regnal year of Amasis, which was during Djekhy's lifetime. The narrative should be taken with a grain of salt: it is likely that Petiese III strove to paint the blackest possible picture of the priests of Amun from al-Hiba.

It began with a fanatical overseer of fields. While this role could be filled by a local official, some acted as national agricultural supervisors and were powerful men acting by order of the king. Their main task was to ensure that the royal granaries were always full. According to the description given by Petiese III, in regnal year 15 of Amasis, this overseer of the fields had noticed something strange about the fields of the temple of Amun in al-Hiba, prompted by information from an otherwise unknown scribe by the name of Payfchauawybastet. On the basis of that information, the overseer launched a fiscal raid he had already been planning:

"There's an island in the possession of the priests of Amun in al-Hiba—484 aruras have been allotted to them, but it is actually one thousand aruras. The statue of Pharaoh Amasis was brought to al-Hiba and NN was appointed as its priest. He allotted 120 aruras to the statue of Pharaoh in al-Hiba, but the statue of Pharaoh that was brought to Heracleopolis was not provided with any field at all." The overseer of fields sailed south. He arrived at the island of al-Hiba and landed at the extreme tip. He had two field surveyors disembark and go around the island all the way. They included the sandy and wooded parts of the island, making a grand total of about 929 aruras. He had the island of al-Hiba confiscated. These 120 aruras of the statue were located at The Field of Sheqeq. He confiscated these as well. The overseer of fields then sent a message to the high officer Manenwakhibre: "The priests of Amun from al-Hiba must come up with four thousand (sacks of) grain (measured with the) forty-hin (measure) as harvest tax for the island that they cultivated." The officer came to al-Hiba and confiscated the granaries. He had all the grain that he found in the granaries of the houses brought to the temple to be kept under lock and key.

Perhaps illustrative of the intricate relations between Pharaoh and Amun is the fact that, instead of accepting the situation, the priests of Amun rushed to the royal palace, guns blazing. They tried to bribe a trusted servant of Amasis with an annual fee of three hundred sacks of grain (twenty-four thousand liters), two hundred hin of ricinus oil (one hundred liters), fifty hin of honey (twenty-five liters), and thirty geese, requesting only that he make sure Pharaoh would allot the island to Amun for an indefinite period of time.

Some intrigues later, the overseer of fields finally found himself standing before the king:

The overseer of fields was taken before Pharaoh. He said: "My great lord! I found an island in the river just across al-Hiba. The scribes of the district told me it encompassed one thousand aruras of fields. I had it measured again and it (actually) encompasses 929 aruras. In the face of Pharaoh! It is not fitting to give this as an offering domain to some god or goddess. It belongs to Pharaoh. It will yield an output of twenty (sacks of) grain with the measure of forty hin for each arura. I then asked the scribes whether this (island) had been allotted to Amun of al-Hiba. They told me that 484½ aruras of it had been allotted to Amun, so I told the priests of Amun: 'Come, and I will make sure that these will be given to you as compensation for your offering domain on the mainland.' But they did not listen to me. As far as Amun of al-Hiba is concerned, I found in his possession an offering domain as if it was a very great house, namely thirty-three and a third (sacks of) grain with the measure of forty hin that are allotted daily to Amun of al-Hiba. From this I can fully maintain them (the priests)."

The court official bribed by the priests of Amun was unable to sway the overseer, who was determined to obtain the fields of Amun on the island of al-Hiba, although he was willing to compensate the priests of Amun for it. This was essentially a business (and political) conflict between the Royal Domain and the Domain of Amun, albeit described by a man who—to put it mildly—was not very keen on the priests of Amun. In other words, the suggestion that the priests of Amun would stop at nothing if their salaries were at stake comes from a highly biased report.

Whether or not Petiese's petition is genuine does not really matter. In Egyptology there are hardly any doubts about the authenticity of P. Rylands 9 (these are confined to specific passages). This papyrus does, however, show what could lie behind the rather dry legal formulary in the lease contracts deposited in the archive of Djekhy & Son. This was a world in which power, wealth, and status were hugely important. A faint echo of this is found in the wisdom text contained in Papyrus Insinger, which we have encountered before (P. Insinger X 5–8):

> The stupid man without protection sleeps in jail. (. . .) Whoever wants to pay for protection will also sleep safely on the street. Whoever pays a bribe in case of litigation is the one who will *always* be in the right.

The origin of the rivalry between the Domain of Amun and the Royal Domain can be traced as far back as the Twentieth Dynasty. Some Egyptologists believe that the economic system in the thirteenth and twelfth centuries BCE was still one of large state and temple landholdings. A small number of sources seem to confirm this: Papyrus Harris (c. 1155 BCE) and Papyrus Wilbour (c. 1140 BCE). It is not much to rely on. P. Harris I—or the Great Papyrus Harris, as it has come to be known because of its forty-two-meter length—records the donations made by Ramesses III to the temples of Egypt during his reign. P. Wilbour is a cadastral survey covering a small area in the middle of Egypt, which apparently records assessments of the yields of arable plots according to their size. Similar texts have recently come to light, like Papyrus Reinhardt from the tenth century BCE, which will eventually allow Egyptologists to paint a more complete and reliable picture. If P. Harris I is to be believed, Ramesses III granted no fewer than 113,433 people to the temples, as well as perhaps 15 percent of the arable land in Egypt. Much of this naturally went to his own mortuary temple at Medinet Habu.

The conflict of ownership and the right of taxation between the Domain of Amun and the Royal Domain described in P. Rylands 9 finds a nice parallel in Papyrus Valençay 1, presumably written at the end of the reign of Ramesses XI, the last pharaoh of that name. In this official letter, the mayor of Elephantine politely but stubbornly refuses to pay taxes to the Domain of the Adoratrice of Amun, claiming that these taxes have consistently been paid to the Treasury of Pharaoh:

[May] Amun praise Menmaaranakhte. The mayor of Elephantine Meryunu sends greeting. In life, prosperity, health and in the praise of Amun-Ra King of Gods. [I say] each day to [Amun-Ra]-Horakhty when he rises and goes to rest, as well as to Khnum, Satis, and Anuqis and all (other) gods of Elephantine: "Keep the chief taxing-master healthy, give him life, prosperity, health, a long lifetime, and a good old age. Give him praise before Amun-Ra King of Gods, his good lord, and before Pharaoh, his good lord."

To wit: the scribe Pachauemdyamun of the Domain of the Adoratrice of Amun came, and he arrived in Elephantine looking for the grain for the Domain of the Adoratrice of Amun. He said to me: "Give one hundred sacks of grain-as-grain." So he said to me, but there are no fields producing that amount. And he also said to me: "They are sought from you because of a *khata* field (i.e., an administrative unit of one thousand square cubits) on the island of Omby." So it was said to me, although I hadn't plowed any *khata* fields on the island of Omby.

As Amun endures, and as the Ruler l.p.h. endures, if a *khata* field on the island of Omby is found that I have plowed, they can demand the grain from me. There is, however, a field of free men who are taking their gold to the Treasury of Pharaoh l.p.h. for the plowing these free men have done, but they have already paid his gold to the Treasury of Pharaoh l.p.h. I have not worked in any field there.

And then they said to me: "There is also the issue of another field in the district of Edfu." But this has not been inundated. Only four aruras of field have been inundated in it and I assigned one man and one yoke to it, and the few patches that were found on it were plowed. So when harvest occurred, they brought me forty sacks of grain-as-grain. I have guarded these, not having laid a finger on a single oipe. I have delivered them to the scribe Pachauemdyamun as forty sacks, whereas I swore a firm oath about them, saying: "I have not laid a finger on any oipe or sack in them." I am sending (this letter) to let the chief taxing-master know.

There is little doubt the New Kingdom tax administration received complaints like these every day. Once these complaints and the subsequent refusal to pay became endemic, partly also as a side effect of the breakdown of central authority, the empire began slowly to fall apart. Herihor's accession as the new pharaoh in Upper Egypt inaugurated the development of two separate ancient Egyptian states.

Relations between these states were mostly peaceful, but eventually the local management and legal cultures diverged, and in Thebes abnormal hieratic became the administrative script—in fact an entirely logical development from late New Kingdom hieratic—while early demotic rose to prominence in Lower Egypt.

The Theban priesthood of Amun was able to achieve this status—some of the high priests assumed royal titles—because the Domain of Amun reportedly owned about 60 percent of all arable temple land and controlled commercial shipping. Several centuries later, the efforts of Psamtik I to regain control of Upper Egypt were thus essentially also aimed at breaking the power of the Domain of Amun.

Into the Flax Business

November–December 555 BCE (Papyrus Louvre E 7844)
In the early winter of 555 BCE, Djekhy and his fellow choachyte Nesamunhotep son of Peteamunip found themselves in the office of the priest

of Amun Khonsuirau son of Hor to lease some flax fields. Only four years earlier Djekhy and Nesamunhotep had quarreled about the choachytes' rights to a tomb in the Theban necropolis (P. Louvre E 7848). Perhaps both men were here to lease a plot of land on behalf of the Theban choachytes' association, or maybe this was a private enterprise. Some months before, Djekhy had harvested the flax from the fields in The Palette of Khonsu, as part of a joint venture of fifteen lessees (P. BM EA 10432). Apparently the flax business suited him.

Apart from the early papyri written between c. 675 and 572 BCE, the archive of Djekhy & Son also contains other documents seemingly unconnected with either Djekhy or Iturech. They cannot have ended up in the archive by chance. Many are closely linked in various ways, dealing with agricultural enterprises sometimes involving choachytes; like the papers of Djekhy & Son, they were written in the middle of the sixth century; and they all come from Thebes. Take, for instance, P. Louvre E 7841, a receipt for the payment of the harvest tax written in the spring of 559 BCE. The text mentions a man called Djekhy, but this is a namesake:

> Regnal year 12, third month of the akhet season under Pharaoh l.p.h. Amasis l.p.h. Entered as delivered by Djekhy son of Ankhkhratnefer and his business partner, delivered into the hand of Petosiris son of Djedhoriufankh, the 1-1/10 of flax from The Source of . . . (?) of the priest and majordomo of the temple of Khonsu Payuyuhor son of Horemakhet, that you have grown with flax from regnal year 11 to regnal year 12. I have received this 1-1/10 of flax. My heart is satisfied with it, there being no remainder. In the writing of Petosiris son of Djedhoriufankh, in person.

The receipt was countersigned by a witness to the delivery. It is remarkable that the man paying the harvest tax has the same name as the archivist. Apparently, after the land lease had been made out in his name, he grew a crop with an anonymous business partner. There are various ways in which this receipt could have ended up in the archive of Djekhy & Son. Perhaps the anonymous business partner was none other than 'our' Djekhy; perhaps he simply kept this receipt for his namesake as a trustee.

To return to the winter of 555 BCE, the lessor Khonsuirau was an official of the almighty Domain of Amun. Amun possessed a vast temple compound in Karnak and Luxor, including an economic department called The God's Offering of Amun. This department was tasked with the annual cultivation of the available land (owned by Amun) after the floods of the Nile had subsided. In the case of P. Louvre E 7844 the lessees Nesamunhotep and Djekhy were ordered by Khonsuirau to grow flax on a number of waste lands. Of the harvest, a third was payable to The God's Offering of Amun, and the lessees took the remainder. They would also supply the oxen for plowing, seedcorn, and manpower. For a man who had no fields of his own, but did have some capital and manpower, this could be a profitable deal. The passage below describes the procedure:

> Regnal year 16, third month of the shemu season under Pharaoh l.p.h. Amasis l.p.h. The priest of Amun Khonsuirau son of Hor has said to the choachyte Nesamunhotep son of Peteamunip and the choachyte Djekhy son of Tesmontu: "I am the one who has said to you: grow flax on the waste lands from regnal year 16 to regnal year 17. When harvest has occurred in regnal year 17, you will give 33.3 percent of all the seed you will harvest to The God's Offering of Amun, in my hand and in the name of the field, and you will take for yourselves 66.7 percent in the name of ox, seedcorn, and man(power). I will let no scribe of the Kalasirians stand before you, except for the 33.3 percent mentioned above."

This is a straightforward land lease, so there is not much more to say about it. We must, however, keep in mind that a written land lease was always special, even if after 2,500 years it is unclear why.

It is interesting to note that the share of the Domain of Amun was apparently to be collected by a scribe of the Kalasirians, a warrior class, who also acted as policemen. Other Theban papyri from the Saite Period suggest that it was more usual for the harvest tax to be collected by scribes of the Domain of Amun.

There is also a puzzling marginal note in this lease: "Remainder: 5-1/32 aruras for which seedcorn has been supplied." This was a small plot; two aruras were about the size of a soccer field. Did this marginal note by the scribe have anything to do with the lease itself? Does it refer to the land actually leased out on this day, or had Nesamunhotep and

Djekhy rented less than the landlord Khonsuirau expected? It seems somehow unlikely that the Domain of Amun would have written a lease contract for such a small field.

The lease contract itself—P. Louvre E 7844—was written by the otherwise unknown scribe Petebastet son of Ankhwennefer. The contract was then countersigned by the landlord. Below his signature, there is the signature of a man called Horsiese son of Petebastet. This was no doubt the son of the scribe, who would be learning the tricks of the trade in his father's office.

Earlier Work

Most of the land leases from the archive of Djekhy & Son became known through their publication in the 1950s. In 1951 the Russian-French demotist Michel Malinine—his father had been the mayor of Moscow during the Russian Revolution, so a hasty flight to France eventually seemed advisable—published an article in the still-leading French Egyptological journal *Revue d'Égyptologie*: "Trois documents de l'époque d'Amasis relatifs au louage de terres." In slightly over twenty pages Malinine was able to explain to a larger audience both what is so difficult about ancient Egyptian land leases and how far he had progressed in deciphering them.

Strangely enough this publication was followed the next year by the equally brilliant *Saite Demotic Land Leases*, a publication of six land leases from the archive of Djekhy & Son by George Hughes—seven if we include P. BM EA 10432. Evidently the war had slowed its publication, because the manuscript was already finished by 1939. The two men had unwittingly been working on the same papyri more or less at the same time.

Hughes, a farmer's son from Nebraska, was an American Egyptologist with a keen eye for early demotic, though better known to some from the acknowledgments of Cecil B. DeMille's 1956 film *The Ten Commandments*. The publication of his dissertation, *Saite Demotic Land Leases*, had been interrupted by the war, when he joined the intelligence service. He would eventually become the professor-director of the Oriental Institute in Chicago as well as an honorary member of the Deutsches Archäologisches Institut and the French Institut d'Égypte, both in Cairo—which was a great honor for an American in those days, when Egyptology was still very much a European affair. He died in 1992.

In the meantime Malinine brought out yet another publication in 1953, a stunning book called *Choix de textes juridiques en hiératique anormal et en démotique.* This contained more texts from the archive of Djekhy & Son, including some that had already been published by George Hughes.[3] Some of Malinine's former students would later publish a volume of plates to accompany his *Choix de textes juridiques,* but not until thirty years later, and it was a disappointment compared to Malinine's first volume.

In 1995 all documents from the archive of Djekhy & Son were published together, some for the first time, in a dissertation from Leiden University: *Abnormal Hieratic and Early Demotic Texts Collected by the Theban Choachytes in the Reign of Amasis: Papyri from the Louvre Eisenlohr Lot.* This was the first time the entire archive was published as a single integral text.

The very few people in this world able to grasp fully the depth of the publications by Malinine and Hughes will be quick to notice that the two men agreed for the most part when it came to reading early demotic texts—and abnormal hieratic P. BM EA 10432 for that matter. What connects them, apart from the atrocious quality of the paper used to print their books in the scarcity that marked the postwar years, is the sheer excellence of their work. Some words may be unread or signs remain unexplained here and there (different ones with each author)— which is only to be expected when publishing texts like these—but owing to these two men it was possible even fifty years ago to gain a deep understanding of the nature of the ancient Egyptian land leasing system, or to be more precise, the ancient Egyptian land leasing system as it applied in Thebes between 556 and 534 BCE. And that's exactly where it remained for fifty years.

It is important to remember too that this understanding is based on just seven documents, all dating back to the time of a single pharaoh, Amasis, who ruled Egypt between 570 and 526 BCE. It is certainly only a tiny fraction of the number of leases created even in the space of those years. If we assume that during his reign about five hundred land leases were written each year, this would amount to twenty-two thousand contracts. Seven of these would be just 0.032 percent of the total. It would therefore seem prudent to treat this material with some reserve. But what about the six abnormal hieratic land leases that were found with the archive of Djekhy & Son: P. Louvre E 7851 recto (front) and verso (back), 7852, 7856 recto and verso, and 7860 (discussed in Chapter 2)? Five of these were published for the first time only recently, in the *Revue d'Égyptologie,* more than a hundred years after Revillout purchased the Eisenlohr collection. P. Louvre E 7860 remains unpublished.

People lucky enough to peruse the papers of the late Francis Llewellyn Griffith and Jaroslav Černý in the Griffith Institute in Oxford—two of the world's best readers of late hieratic—will find photos of these papyri, but not a single transcription into hieroglyphs. Michel Malinine, who published most of the papyri from the archive of Djekhy & Son, regularly referred to passages in P. Louvre E 7851–7856 in his notes. He was clearly working on them, but he never published them. The reason they remained unpublished for so long is actually very simple: nobody could properly read them.

It is worth making a slight digression to look at how Egyptologists work with the texts they study. When deciphering abnormal hieratic and early demotic texts, the signs on the original sources must be 'translated' into a format that is comprehensible to Egyptologists, particularly since there are only a few Egyptologists who read early demotic, let alone abnormal hieratic (the latter is read by perhaps ten Egyptologists worldwide).

There are two main ways to effect this 'translation.' We can transcribe the signs into hieroglyphs. We can also transliterate them into standard European consonants (the Egyptians wrote no vowels, but there are many tricks to pronounce ancient Egyptian). The difference between a transcription and a transliteration is that a transcription tells the reader that you have actually understood all the individual signs and connected sign groups (ligatures), whereas a transliteration avoids this problem by simply ignoring it. The real diehards use both a transcription and a transliteration in their publications, because the transcription shows what they saw, but a transliteration is much handier to use in the notes to a text.

To complicate things, some publications refer to a transliteration as transcription, and different countries have different transliteration systems. An anecdote sometimes heard in Egyptological circles illustrates the problem quite nicely: Ask a German, an Englishman, and a Frenchman to write a book about the camel. In five months the Frenchman will come up with a booklet that elegantly describes the world of the camel: *Mes aventures fantastiques et héroïques sur le dos d'un chameau extraordinaire.* It will be a brilliant but wafer-thin publication that fills the reader with awe, but provides none of the simple, everyday facts about the camel that the reader had hoped to learn. The Englishman will work hard for a year and write a thorough book describing the camel in great detail, including types, behavior, and statistics: *Everything You Need to Know about Camels*. The German will toil long and hard for half a decade. He will deliver his *Das Kamel* in four bulky volumes, including every imaginable detail about the camel. Unfortunately his book is unreadable because of the five thousand footnotes the author crammed into it to ensure that no detail, however small, was overlooked.

The competing transliteration systems are much the same. Attempts were made in the 1980s to arrive at a uniform transliteration system for demotic, but so far they have been in vain. Since the rise of modern linguistics even more peculiarities have crept into these systems. For instance, Egyptologists have for generations transliterated the Egyptian sign for the combination 'ch' (as in rich) as a t with a stroke underneath: *ṯ*. Nowadays, however, there are also Egyptologists who favor the use of *č* for the same sound, because this apparently is linguistically more correct. Since there is absolutely no difference between the pronunciation of *ṯ* and *č*, perhaps the time could have been better spent on unifying the various transliteration systems.

Lease, Harvest, and Tax

P. Louvre E 7844 was written in November or December 555 BCE. Most land leases would be arranged in autumn, from September onward. By then the floods of the Nile had subsided and the fields were ready for plowing and sowing, so this was the best time to do business. The landlord usually retained a quarter or a third of the harvest. The difference was probably determined by the quality of the land, the crop, the distance lessees had to travel to get there, the amount of work and water needed, who provided the plowing oxen and seedcorn, and so on.

Naturally, there were all sorts of exceptions and variants. In P. Louvre E 7833 from 535 BCE, the landlord receives five-sixths of the harvest, and in P. Louvre E 7839 from 534 BCE he gets it all, although this document may no longer properly be called a land lease, since apparently the 'lessee' was working the land to repay a debt. The landlord in this case was Iturech, the second owner of the archive of Djekhy & Son.

Then there was the harvest tax of the Domain of Amun. A number of the abnormal hieratic land lease contracts from the archive of Djekhy & Son refer to a tenth.[4] In P. Louvre E 7845A from 554 BCE, in exchange for allowing the lessee to work the land, the landlord retains a quarter of the harvest, "the harvest tax of the Domain of Amun being included." We can infer from this that the harvest tax was in any case less than 25 percent. We also regularly come across the 10 percent figure in the early abnormal hieratic land leases, and we know from the Bible that a tenth of the harvest—the fruit tithe—had to be paid to the temple. It would thus be reasonable to conclude that the harvest tax of the Domain of Amun would also have been 10 percent of the total harvest. In Europe this tithe, as the harvest tax became known, was introduced under Charlemagne. The proceeds were used to care for the poor, but also to pay church authorities and buy real estate. In Germany this tithe tax is still known as the *Kirchensteuer* (church tax).

A Major Deal

July–August 554 BCE (Papyrus Louvre E 7845A)

Djekhy did well by growing flax—or more probably having flax grown by sublessees or employees. That is why the priest of Amun-Ra King of Gods Psamtik son of Ankhpakhrat—the same man who had leased out the large flax fields in The Palette of Khonsu in the winter of 556–555 BCE, recorded in P. BM EA 10432—reappears in the archive the following summer. This time Psamtik also used the prestigious-looking title 'priest of the great Shu, foremost of the Benben'[5] and even included the name of his father's father, Efau.

Outside it was midsummer and stifling hot—temperatures could easily rise to forty degrees Celsius—but the scribe was obviously in a good mood, which we may infer from the fact that, apart from Psamtik's lengthy title, he would also write a beautiful-looking contract on this day. Before him stood the choachyte Chayutayudeny son of Peteamunip and Hemes, one of the fifteen lessees of land in The Palette of Khonsu the year before (P. BM EA 10432). On this day Chayutayudeny and Psamtik closed a deal about the cultivation of a vast piece of land:

> Regnal year 17, third month of the peret season under Pharaoh l.p.h. Amasis l.p.h. The priest of Amun-Ra King of Gods and the priest of the great Shu, foremost of the Benben Psamtik son of Ankhpakhrat son of Efau, has said to the choachyte of the valley Chayutayudeny son of Peteamunip, whose mother is Hemes: "I have leased to you my fields in the Domain of Amun in the southern area to the west of Thebes, in the . . . Specification: my field which is called The Palette of Khonsu—its south being the drain of Hapy the Great (the Nile),

its north being the fields of the Adoratrice of the God, its west being the fields of the Adoratrice of the God, and its east being the water of Na-Pe. I have leased them to you together with my fields of the mortuary foundation of vizier Pamy—their south being the fields of the Adoratrice of the God, their north being the fields of the singer of the interior of Amun Esekheb, their west being the fields of the . . . scribe and their east being the the fields of the Adoratrice of the God, that have in turn been leased to me to till them from regnal year 17 to regnal year 18 for their remainder in flax, for their 25 percent, the harvest tax of the Domain of Amun being included. When harvest has occurred in regnal year 18 you will give me 25 percent of all grain, of all the flax you will bring from them, and I will make sure the scribes of the Domain of Amun will be far from you regarding their harvest tax of the Domain of Amun. The scribes of the Domain of Amun will measure my fields in my name, and the mismanagement by the cultivator they will find on them, you will have to pay it to me from your share of the harvest according to what will be determined, and you will leave my fields in regnal year 18."

The date on which this lease was concluded is unusual. (It must be remembered, however, that there are only about thirteen land leases left from the Late Period, and much of what we have known about them for the past fifty years has been based on only seven of these, as published by George Hughes and Michel Malinine [see above, "Earlier Work"].) In Thebes in the sixth century BCE, a land lease was generally concluded in autumn, after the floodwaters had subsided enough that the arable land could be measured and staked off for cultivation. This contract between Psamtik and Chayutayudeny, however, was written between 8 July and 7 August 554 BCE, which was midsummer. This might be explained by the fact that Chayutayudeny had leased land in the same area the previous year, as part of a joint venture of fifteen lessees, also including Djekhy. The harvest in 555 BCE must have been good, so that they were eager to repeat this success. Chayutayudeny would never be able to cultivate The Palette of Khonsu on his own. Above, we calculated that this field must have been enormous to sustain fifteen lessees, possibly measuring one hundred aruras (fifty soccer fields or twenty-five hectares). Moreover, in the summer of 554 BCE Chayutayudeny also leased fields connected with the mortuary cult of vizier Pamy. These would have been fields of very high quality—nobody would dare allot bad fields to the mortuary cult of such a highly placed official—which may have been another reason for Chayutayudeny to call on Psamtik earlier than usual. The size of these lands may provide a clue to the connection between this lease and the archive of Djekhy & Son. It suggests that Chayutayudeny concluded this contract on behalf of the same group we met in P. BM EA 10432, and maybe even a larger one. Since the contract was found with the archive, it is likely that Djekhy either kept it in his capacity as trustee or was again among the lessees.

Egyptian land leases often mention the neighboring plots in order precisely to demarcate the area that is the subject of the lease. As evident in P. BM EA 10432, where the land was referred to only by the collective name The Palette of Khonsu, this appears not to have been a universal practice. P. Louvre E 7845A is more conventional. It says explicitly that the leased land was bordered on two sides by waterways, The Drain of Hapy the Great (a canal connecting to the Nile) and The Water of Na-Pe (in which Pe probably stands for the city of Buto in the Delta). The contract also clarifies that The Palette of Khonsu was enclosed by fields belonging to the Adoratrice of Amun, the highest priestess in Egypt.

When this lease was concluded, the Adoratrice of Amun was princess Ankhnesneferibra, the daughter of Psamtik II. She had been adopted in 595 BCE by Nitocris, the previous Adoratrice and daughter of Psamtik I. The institution of the Adoratrice of Amun was clearly used by the Saite kings from the north to strengthen their hold on the powerful priesthood of Amun in Upper Egypt. Nitocris died around 586 BCE. She was succeeded by Ankhnesneferibra, who in turn adopted Nitocris II, the daughter of Amasis. Ankhnesneferibra was to remain Adoratrice up to the conquest of Egypt by the Persians. Whether the fields of the Adoratrice mentioned in this contract were used for the cult of the deceased Nitocris I or to maintain the living Adoratrice Ankhnesneferibra doesn't really matter. These would be fields of the highest quality. No wonder the choachyte Chayutayudeny had been in a hurry to lease this land.

The conditions of the lease contract are clear. The landlord Psamtik would receive 25 percent of the harvest, including the harvest tax of the Domain of Amun. Although he refers to the land as "my fields," he also states that the fields "have in turn been leased to me from regnal year 17 to regnal year 18." It is therefore possible that he was acting as an official of The God's Offering of Amun, and that Chayutayudeny

Approximate location of The Palette of Khonsu, according to P. Louvre E 7845A:

N ↑	The fields of the singer of the interior of Amun		
The fields of the . . . scribe	The fields of the mortuary foundation of vizier Pamy*	The fields of the Adoratrice of God	The Water of Na-Pe
	The fields of the Adoratrice of God	The Palette of Khonsu*	
	The Drain of Hapy the Great		

The fields leased in July–August 554 BCE are marked *

was in fact leasing land that belonged to the economic department of the Domain of Amun. Psamtik and Chayutayudeny also agreed that the land would be measured—i.e., the harvest would be estimated—by the scribes of the Domain of Amun in Psamtik's name. If the harvest was lower than expected due to Chayutayudeny's mismanagement, he would have to make up the shortfall. The final clause of this contract occurs only sporadically in Egyptian lease contracts. After the harvest in regnal year 18 of Amasis, Chayutayudeny would have to abandon the fields. Since no two land lease contracts are the same and conditions were tailored to the occasion, it seems that Psamtik had experienced some trouble in the past with lessees refusing to give up the fields after their contract had ended.

The lease was signed by the scribe Petehor son of Ankhefenamun whom we only know from this contract. The Theban landlord Psamtik—named after the pharaohs from the Delta—also signed, in abnormal hieratic.

A Late Payment?

29 October 552 BCE (Papyrus Louvre E 7847)
Somewhere in the agricultural year 554–553 BCE Djekhy had also found time to do business with the otherwise unknown Pakhorkhonsu son of Namenekhamunip and Mrs. Hetepamun. His prestigious title Servant of the Place of Truth is likewise unknown. There are references to a Place of Truth in relation to cities like Memphis and Abydos. Some Egyptologists have suggested the term could refer to the Serapeum and the

tomb of Osiris, respectively. In the New Kingdom—hundreds of years earlier—the Place of Truth in the Theban necropolis was the Valley of the Kings. The Servant of the Place of Truth was a title reserved for the workmen of Deir al-Medina who cut out and decorated the royal tombs. Perhaps over the centuries it had become the name for a specific part of the Theban necropolis, like the Assasif, where many tombs from the Late Period were found, or the necropolis area as a whole. Or perhaps Pakhorkhonsu was just a choachyte who had simply come across this New Kingdom title in the Theban necropolis, a place teeming with graffiti and ancient inscriptions.

On 29 October 552 BCE, Pakhorkhonsu and Djekhy found themselves before the overseer of the necropolis Petehorresne son of Peteamunip. Petehorresne's son Peteamunip—who, we recall, was an apprentice in his father's business—was also present and would sign Pakhorkhonsu's statement as a witness (see figure 6). Apparently Pakhorkhonsu had quarreled with Djekhy about a payment the latter owed him for the field they had cultivated in 554–553 BCE. This field was called The Land of the Servant of the Place of Truth, so it must have been in Pakhorkhonsu's possession. Well over a year later the account still hadn't been settled, which is probably why both men were here today in the office of the overseer of the necropolis:

> Regnal year 19, second month of the shemu season under Pharaoh l.p.h. Amasis l.p.h. The servant of the place of truth Pakhorkhonsu son of Namenekhamunip, whose mother is Hetepamun, has said to the choachyte Djekhy son of Tesmontu: "You have satisfied my heart with my share of business partner for my land, which is called The Land of the Servant of the Place of Truth, the south of which being the access to The Land (of) the Hand of God, that I cultivated, you being my business partner from regnal year 17 to regnal year 18. I have received it. My heart is satisfied with it, there being no remainder." In the writing of the overseer of the necropolis Petehorresne <son of> Peteamunip. In the writing of Peteamunip son of Petehorresne.

The scribe Petehorresne and Djekhy were old acquaintances. Djekhy would visit his office from time to time as a result of his business activities. In 568 BCE Petehorresne drew up a quitclaim for Djekhy (P. Louvre E 7861). In 559 BCE he wrote P. Louvre E 7848 after the quarrel about the choachytes' rights to service the mummies in a tomb that may have been owned by Djekhy and his business partners.

Petehorresne was trained in the local Theban scribal tradition, meaning that he wrote abnormal hieratic. We have, however, seen above how he adapted the early demotic formula, "You have satisfied my heart"—never seen in abnormal hieratic—for his own use in P. Louvre E 7861: "You have satisfied my heart with your oath in the presence of Khonsuemwasneferhotep, from today onward," and here in P. Louvre E 7847: "You have satisfied my heart with my share of business partner for my land." He was so happy with this *trouvaille* that he also taught it to his son Peteamunip. In a quitclaim written by the latter in 547 BCE for the choachyte Rery, Djekhy's brother, the same formula—creatively adapted—is seen once again (P. Cairo CG 30657): "You have satisfied my heart with all things." In this manner early demotic, imported from the Delta, slowly but surely gained a foothold in the abnormal hieratic tradition in distant Thebes.

The Hand of God
The southern neighbor of the field owned by Pakhorkhonsu gave access to another plot called The Land (of) the Hand of God. The Hand of God dates as far back as the Middle Kingdom. It was mainly associated with Hathor, the goddess of dance and sex. The ivory and wooden castanets used by female dancers would be hand-shaped, subtly stressing the erotic connotation still associated with dance today. In the Twenty-fifth Dynasty the title Hand of God was added to the epithets of the Adoratrice of Amun, the daughter of the king and the highest priestess in the land. It was also a title that left very little to the imagination. In one of the Egyptian cosmogonies the god Atum is standing on the primeval hill, creating a divine ennead (the nine principal gods) through masturbation. In the Theban cosmogony this role was taken over by Amun. The Adoratrice of Amun—the Hand of God—in turn was the bride of Amun playing a vital part in this (ritual) creation.

6

Grain
Iturech 550–536 BCE

The Second Generation

After 550 BCE (Papyrus Louvre E 7854)

Around the middle of the sixth century BCE, Djekhy son of Tesmontu vanishes from the stage. We do not know whether he died or was pensioned off to participate in the family business only from a distance. By this time he would have been at least forty years old, which was rather elderly in Saite Egypt. Many friends from his youth would probably be dead by now. Chances are that Djekhy himself—if he was still alive—was suffering from the guinea worm disease (dracunculiasis) caused by drinking contaminated water, or the omnipresent bilharzia, which would eventually lead to abdominal pains, coughs, diarrhea, fever, fatigue, or genital sores. If he was lucky, he would only be tormented by the usual ailments associated with old age, like extreme tooth decay, partly caused by the ancient Egyptian staple food, sandy bread.

Whatever befell Djekhy, we know that the official records of the Theban choachytes' association (P. Louvre E 7840) written ten years later do not mention his name. His son Iturech had taken over Djekhy & Son and had become the new owner of the archive. On the basis of what we know from other sources, it is likely that Iturech was regularly involved in the family business from his tenth birthday onward. Djekhy would have taken him to the meetings held by the choachytes' association, not only to learn about the mores, but also to meet his future colleagues and business partners. A Ptolemaic papyrus from the choachytes' milieu mentions ten as the the right age to start a career as a choachyte. At the age of sixteen boys were expected to become full members of the choachytes' association. Documents like P. Louvre

E 7861 and 7848—both dealing with Djekhy's business quarrels—would have been useful tools for Djekhy to teach his son how to navigate the ancient Egyptian business world. We know from their business dealings that both men were skilled at accounting. We do not know, however, whether either Djekhy or Iturech could write. Literacy rates were very low in ancient Egypt; perhaps only 3 percent of the population (some say only 1 percent) was literate, which is a percentage in line with the literacy rate in the early Middle Ages. The archive holds one signature by Iturech, on the verso of P. Louvre E 7832, but this proves only that he could write his own name. The quality of that signature, however, which is almost indistinguishable from the writing by a professional scribe, suggests that Iturech could indeed read and write.

Figure 7. Signature of Iturech son of Djekhy on the back of P. Louvre E 7832. Did he personally sign the contract in which he bought a son in 539 BCE? [Courtesy Musée du Louvre; author's facsimile]

P. Louvre E 7854—an official letter written after 550 BCE[1]—shows that Iturech had now taken over the family business. He is mentioned in this papyrus together with his brother Khausenmin, who plays a very minor role in the archive of Djekhy & Son after this. Khausenmin was also a choachyte. He is listed twice in the records of the choachytes' association (P. Louvre E 7840 II 16 and IV 14). The second mention in column IV of P. Louvre E 7840 is especially interesting, because this is a list of all the people who had become members of the association from regnal year 27 of Amasis onward. Iturech appears second in this list, Khausenmin only twelfth, and their uncle Rery fourteenth, even though he was older than the two brothers. Is this some indirect proof that Iturech had taken over the position of his father Djekhy as the new paterfamilias?

P. Louvre E 7854 is over 2,500 years old. A common problem with old letters like these (and many younger sources for that matter) is that we lack a solid context, which means that the sender, addressee, and contents always remain slightly hazy. Not so in P. Louvre E 7854. We know both the sender and addressee well from other documents kept in the archive of Djekhy & Son. We even understand most of what is being written here. As is to be expected, the letter starts with a standard formula to wish the addressee well: "Memo by Djedkhonsuiufankh son of Rery to the priest of Amun Petemestu. May Ra give that his life be long!"

The archive of Djekhy & Son contains four receipts for the harvest tax of the Domain of Amun: P. Louvre E 7834, 7835, 7838, and 7842. They were written between 540 and 536 BCE by the scribe of the mat Petemestu son of Horsiese. These receipts were always countersigned by a number of witnesses. Three of the four were signed by a witness called Djedkhonsuiufankh son of Rery, no doubt the same man who wrote (or dictated) P. Louvre E 7854. It thus makes sense to equate the receiver of the letter, the priest of Amun Petemestu, with the scribe of the mat Petemestu who wrote the four receipts. But can we be certain? The difficulty—and difficulties like these tend to become inflated to almost mythical proportions in Egyptology—is that the receiver of the letter is a priest of Amun called Petemestu, whereas the Petemestu who wrote the receipts for Iturech is a scribe of the mat. This may mean they were different people, or it may simply reflect flattery in the hope of a favor: Djedkhonsuiufankh needed Petemestu to write a receipt for the harvest tax paid by the choachyte Iturech and his brother Khausenmin:

> As far as Khausenmin son of Djekhy and his brother Iturech are concerned, they have paid their emmer to the granary. May Petemestu grant me this favor and have a receipt made out for them.

Note that Khausenmin is mentioned earlier than his brother Iturech, even though the latter either would take over or had already taken over the family enterprise Djekhy & Son. The letter continues with some obscure phrases that can be interpreted to mean that Djedkhonsuiufankh refers to Petemestu as 'Your Grace.' The deference suggests Petemestu was senior in rank to the letter-writer Djedkhonsuiufankh, but this impression is shattered by what looks like an official order from Djedkhonsuiufankh: "Have no receipt made out for anyone else without letting me know in advance."

P. Louvre E 7854 is a relatively straightforward official letter and so teaches us a number of important things. The actual receipts for the harvest tax in the archive of Djekhy & Son show that Petemestu, who wrote these receipts, and Djedkhonsuiufankh, who wrote this letter (and who also countersigned three of the receipts written by Petemestu), usually worked in the same office when the harvest tax of the Domain of Amun was paid. This may have been a little office near or in the granary of the Domain of Amun in the district of Coptos. It is sometimes presumed that the district of Coptos extended to Qurna, so this granary may have been located just north of Thebes on the west bank of the Nile. It is where the taxpayers came to deliver the tithe on their harvest.

In this particular case, Petemestu was clearly absent, and it was Djedkhonsuiufankh who received the payment of the harvest tax and who was obliged to send a special letter to ask Petemestu to write out a receipt. These may seem irrelevant details at first sight, but they make the difference between a 2,500-year-old letter that—exciting though it may be—means little to us and a 2,500-year-old letter in which all the persons mentioned are identifiable and can be fitted into a clear context, in this case the ancient Egyptian tax administration. We are in fact observing the mechanism of bureaucratic Saite Egypt from within, and we can see that it operated like clockwork.

Your Grace or Dung?

Papyrus Louvre E 7854 was published in a scientific edition for the first time in 1985, exactly one hundred years after the archive of Djekhy & Son was bought in Egypt. Despite the fact that it was published in the leading scientific *Journal of Egyptian Archaeology* (1985, issue 71), and apparently also subjected to the critical scrutiny of the brilliant American demotist George Hughes, this publication was not a great success.

Let us consider the following passage (the square brackets [. . .] indicate a lacuna):

[Communication from Djed]khonsuiufankh son of Rery before the prophet of Amun Petemestu. May Ra cause your lifetime to be long. [Concerning Pet]emin, the son of Djekhy together with Iturech, his eldest brother: they have paid their emmer to the granary. May [Petem]estu do for me this favor concerning them: may they make their payment for our dung. I know that the choachytes . . . May it be great pertaining to our dung. If not, the dung becomes theirs. If it (?) . . . with you, do not let them make payment to another person without letting me know. Written by the servant [Djedkhonsuiufankh in year xx, month of xx day x +] 2.

Unfortunately that is not what the papyrus says. Apart from the usual problems connected with reading and interpreting early demotic, the essence of this official letter is actually as follows:

[Memo by Djedkhonsu]iufankh son of Rery to the priest of Amun Petemestu. May Ra give that his life be long! [As far as Khaus]enmin son of Djekhy and his brother Iturech are concerned, they have paid their emmer to the granary. May [Petem]estu grant me this favor and have a receipt made out for them. Your Grace knows that the choachytes [. . .] this. May it grow in the hand of Your Grace. If this . . . hadn't happened, I would have [. . .] before you. Have no receipt made out for anyone else without letting me know in advance. Written by the servant [in regnal year . . .] month of the shemu season, day 9.

Is this the same letter? What has been translated as 'Your Grace' is in fact a free rendering of a rare ancient Egyptian expression that translated literally means 'your enemies.' There is no doubt about the rendering 'Your Grace.' In the 1985 edition the word for 'enemies' was mistakenly read as the word for 'dung,' changing an official letter about the payment of the harvest tax and the writing of a receipt into a rather obscure letter about dung.

There is a worse mistake. The 1985 author knew about the connection between P. Louvre E 7854, P. BM EA 10113, 10432, P. Louvre E 7844, 7845, 7855, and 7861. He was also aware that these all belonged to the archive of Djekhy & Son. Yet he chose to read the (damaged) name of Iturech's brother as Petemin instead of Khausenmin. This in turn led him to ascribe P. Louvre E 7854 to an entirely different early demotic archive from Thebes.

Reading early demotic and abnormal hieratic requires much patience. It is no coincidence that neither Griffith, nor Černý, nor Malinine ever published the abnormal hieratic land leases from the reign of Taharqa that are related to this archive: P. Louvre E 7851–7856 (see above, "Earlier Work"). They preferred not to publish rather than to publish hastily and haphazardly. The author of the *editio princeps* of P. Louvre E 7854 could, and perhaps should, have followed their example, all the more so because the plate in the original publication by Eisenlohr and Revillout, *Corpus Papyrorum Aegypti* (1885–1902), was not reliable enough for a publication.

Some notorious examples are shown below in figure 8 (right). The left column shows the facsimiles of the same passages made from the original papyrus in the Louvre.

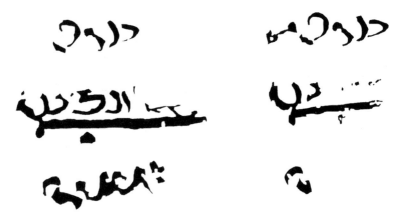

Figure 8. What happens if you do not check the original papyrus: facsimiles made on the original (left) and the 1885–1902 *héliogravure* by Eisenlohr and Revillout [Courtesy Musée du Louvre; author's facsimile]

More than Ten Hectares of Land?

2 September–2 October 540 BCE (Papyrus Louvre E 7842, 7835, 7838, and 7834)

Like his father Djekhy before him, Iturech spread the company risks. He was often seen in the Theban necropolis bringing funerary offerings to his clients, or maybe watching his employees do it for him from a distance. Just like his father, he was not only a funerary service provider, but had entered the agriculture business as well. As far as we know, Djekhy had mainly been active in flax, whereas Iturech focused on growing emmer. The archive of Djekhy & Son contains four receipts for the 10 percent harvest tax of the Domain of Amun. Three of these were written between 540 and 536 BCE. They undoubtedly concern the same field:

- P. Louvre E 7842 (540 BCE): 5 sacks and 1-1/6 oipe
- P. Louvre E 7835 (537 BCE): 5 sacks and 1-1/6 oipe
- P. Louvre E 7838 (536 BCE): 6 sacks and 3-1/6 oipe

In these three years the harvest tax for this field varied between four hundred and five hundred liters of grain per year, allowing us to calculate that the field itself would probably have measured 5.5 aruras, or more than 1.5 hectares. According to the scribe of these receipts this field was located in the west, or more precisely "in the west of the high land The Stable." Other papyri refer to this area as The Stable of the Milk Can of Amun. It lay to the north of Thebes, somewhere in the district of Coptos on the west bank of the Nile. Judging by the name, this is where Amun's cattle grazed.

In 1985 the American demotist Eugene Cruz-Uribe published a neat little volume called *Saite and Persian Demotic Cattle Documents: A Study in Legal Forms and Principles in Ancient Egypt,* in which he collected all contracts connected with cattle in the Late Period. Another Egyptologist used this material to identify the cattle brands, like 'the crocodile,' 'the falcon,' 'the obelisk,' and 'the milk can.'[2] The cows grazing in The Stable of the Milk Can of Amun would have been branded with a mark indicating that fact.

In this period cows often also had names. Most of these are standard personal names like Setayretbin ('The evil eye is removed') or Eserashe ('Isis is happy'). There is, however, one name in P. Berlin 15831 (464 BCE) that is so unusual it baffled the Egyptologist who drew up the list of cows' names (the same, by the way, who collected the cattle brands): the name is Tarumumy, and to say it aloud gives a clue to its meaning, and to the distance between a scholar's study and an actual field. Anyone who has seen, or rather heard, a cow at close range will recognize this as an ono-matopeia. These occur much more often in ancient Egyptian than people realize. One of the Egyptian words for cat, for instance, was *miu,* and pigs were called *reru.* One of the nicest onomatopeias is the word *petpet,* which was used to describe the trampling of enemies by the king. The name Tarumumy—which translates as 'She of Rumumy'—was probably an imitation of the sound the calf's mother made.

But to return to Iturech: this 1.5-hectare field was not the only plot he owned in The Stable of the Milk Can of Amun. It remains unclear, however, whether this is the plot he rented to the cattle keeper of Montu Petemontu son of Pwakhamun, who was acting on behalf of a number of business associates (P. Louvre E 7836, 536 BCE). The land rented to Petemontu, referred to as Taseby (a name no one has been able to translate), is described as being in the high land of The Stable of the Milk Can of Amun. The contract states that Iturech had received it "for the mouth of the priest of Amun-Ra King of Gods Inaros son of Teskhonsu," in other words, to maintain the mortuary cult of the deceased priest. It lay to the east of The Lamp Land of Khonsu, which had been devoted to Khonsu by some pious believer. Its harvest was used to keep a lamp burning in the temple of the god, like a candle in a Roman Catholic church.

Iturech and the cattle keeper Petemontu agreed to divide the harvest into two parts and to pay the harvest tax of the Domain of Amun together. After the tax had been paid, each would receive 45 percent of the total harvest, meaning that Iturech would receive significantly more than the average quarter or third paid to a landlord.

The archive of Djekhy & Son also contains a tax receipt from an earlier transaction between the same men. Somewhere between 4 May and 3 June 536 BCE, Iturech came to pay the harvest tax not just for his 1.5-hectare plot in The Stable of the Milk Can of Amun (P. Louvre E 7838), but also for another field in the same area (P. Louvre E 7834).[3] For the second field, he paid the harvest tax together with Petemontu and his brother Ituru (for a direct translation, see above, "P. Louvre E 7834 and 7838"). According to the scribe, this payment was for the harvest tax of a field they had cultivated from regnal year 34 to 35 (of Amasis). The partners had to pay thirty-seven sacks of grain, about 2,960 liters. Since the harvest tax was 10 percent of the total yield, we can extrapolate that this field produced approximately 29,600 liters of grain. And if we set the estimated yield at ten sacks (eight hundred liters) per arura, we can calculate that the approximate size of this second field was about nine hectares.

From a logistical point of view it would have been quite a challenge to harvest both plots and to transport the grain—more than thirty thousand liters would have weighed about fifteen tons—to all the stakeholders involved: the scribes of the Domain of Amun in the district of Coptos, the landlord Iturech, the lessee Petemontu, and Petemontu's business partners. If we set a donkey load at a reasonable seventy-five kilograms, this combined harvest would require two hundred donkeys. The most convenient means for bulk transport, however, was the river Nile. This was a good harvest if we compare it to the figures of the annual and festival offerings made in the temples of Ramesses II and III in the New Kingdom, which amounted to almost one million liters of grain and would have weighed five hundred tons. Viewed in this context, Iturech's harvest tax alone would have accounted for 3 percent of the annual expenditure of these temples. This was a sizable harvest.

Iturech's apparent ownership of the nine hectares of arable land referred to in P. Louvre E 7834 does raise a serious question: was it normal to give nine hectares of land to a choachyte—whether permanently or on loan—in return for the mortuary cult for just one priest of Amun, even if this person belonged to the famous Besmut family (see further below)? It seems like a very large payment. Or was this land actually also allotted to the cult of that priest's entire family, including parents, grandparents, brothers and sisters, cousins and nephews, sons and daughters? Might it be possible that Iturech actually received fewer than nine hectares from the Besmut family, and the figure actually refers to his total landholding, some of which he had owned already?

All we know for certain from the tax receipts in the archive of Djekhy & Son is that Iturech paid the harvest tax for two separate plots, one measuring 1.5 hectares (P. Louvre E 7838) and the other nine hectares (P. Louvre E 7834). Somehow it seems unlikely that Petemontu would have a written lease made out for a field of only 1.5 hectares, agree to the landlord retaining 45 percent of the yield, and still have to divide his 45-percent share (only about two thousand liters of grain) with other business partners. The solution that seems to make the most sense is the one suggested above: that Iturech owned a total of nine hectares, only part of which was received as payment from the Besmut family. If that is the case, we may not be able to infer the size of the field transferred in P. Louvre E 7836 directly from the harvest tax receipts. The field would probably have been larger than 1.5 hectares (too small for a written lease) but smaller than nine (an unreasonably large payment for one priest's funerary cult).

We do not know exactly how the harvest tax was estimated in provincial Egypt in the sixth century BCE. Land leases, however, regularly contain a clause saying: "The scribes of the Domain of Amun will measure the fields in my name," indicating that the scribes themselves visited the fields to estimate the harvest. Among the officials of the Domain of Amun there would of course have been farmers' sons who would know how to estimate the size of the harvest on the basis of such factors as the quality and state of the field, the distance to the water, the weather, earlier estimates for the same field, old tax receipts, and so on. Trust was good, but checks were better.

These scribes of Amun were the result of a refined bureaucratic machine that had been applying this wisdom for centuries. There would be plenty of times when their presence was warranted, for instance when the floods had subsided and the fields had to be staked off, or when the grain had come up. The scribes measured the fields using ropes that were crowned with the ram's head of Amun to show that they had been officially calibrated. Measuring the fields when the grain had come up was the perfect time for the scribes to adjust their earlier estimate. Any other stage in the process—harvest, transport, threshing—offered landowners and lessees an opportunity for fraud.

We do not know to what extent Iturech was personally involved in raising the crops on his fields, except that he concluded some land leases in person and also came to pay the harvest tax of the Domain of Amun to the scribes of Amun in the district of Coptos. It is understandable that he would have liked to keep track of his interests, especially when his presence was advisable from a business point of view. One can imagine that Iturech would have been present to supervise some of the stages of the cultivation of his fields in person, for instance:

- when staking off the arable plots after the Nile had subsided;
- when plowing and sowing his more than ten (!) hectares of land;
- when the harvest was estimated by the scribes of Amun on the basis of the standing crop, perhaps the same scribes who wrote and countersigned the tax receipts;
- during harvest and threshing; and
- during transport to the threshing floor, to the office of the scribes of Amun, to his own granary, and to the granary of business associates.

This doesn't mean that Iturech always had to be present in person. Ancient Egyptian businessmen, like their modern counterparts, relied on representatives and agents to look after their interests.

The harvest tax receipts that Petemestu drew up for Iturech were signed by witnesses in the order listed in Table 5.

Most of these witnesses are known from a number of tax receipts, suggesting that they probably all worked in the same granary office of Amun in the district of Coptos. The fact that the witnesses' names appear in the same order in both P. Louvre E 7838 and 7834, the receipts made out for the two fields owned by Iturech in May or June 536 BCE, suggests that these receipts were written first and witnessed later. Petemestu and Djedkhonsuiufankh are of course known from P. Louvre E 7854 (see above, "The Second Generation"). Two of the other witnesses are also known from other sources.

Table 5. Harvest tax receipts

P. Louvre E 7842	P. Louvre E 7835	P. Louvre E 7838	P. Louvre E 7834
c. Sept. 540 BCE	c. July 537 BCE	c. May 536 BCE	c. May 536 BCE
Petosiris son of Khedebkhonsuirbin	Khonsuirtais son of Djedmutiufankh	Khonsuirtais son of Djedmutiufankh	Khonsuirtais son of Djedmutiufankh
Horwedja son of Wennefer son of Horwedja, the scribe of the Domain of Amun in the district of Coptos	Nesamun son of Nesiah	Djedkhonsuiufankh son of Rery	Djedkhonsuiufankh son of Rery
Djedbastetiufankh son of Psamtikmenekh	Neswennefer son of Sobekemhat	Petehorresne son of Khedebkhonsuirbin	Petehorresne son of Khedebkhonsuirbin
	Horwedja son of Wennefer, the scribe of the Domain of Amun in the district of Coptos	Horwedja son of Wennefer, the scribe of the Domain of Amun in the district of Coptos	Horwedja son of Wennefer, the scribe of the Domain of Amun in the district of Coptos
	Djedkhonsuiufankh son of Rery	Petosiris son of Khedebkhonsuirbin	Petosiris son of Khedebkhonsuirbin
		Neswennefer son of Sobekemhat	Neswennefer son of Sobekemhat

In P. Louvre E 7842, Horwedja, himself a scribe of the Domain of Amun in the district of Coptos, signs not just his own name, but also those of his father and grandfather, who was his namesake. All three men had been scribes of the Domain of Amun. In 587 BCE grandfather Horwedja bought a plot of twenty-two aruras—more than five hectares—in the same Domain of Amun in the district of Coptos. At the end of the seventh century BCE this land had been in the possession of a god's father Petosiris son of Wenamun, who transferred it to his daughter Nitocris, a singer of the interior of Amun and so someone of elevated rank. Nitocris died before 587 BCE, and the land was passed on to a man called Neskhonsu son of Pakhar, a scribe and servant of the royal palace. This Neskhonsu then sold the land to grandfather Horwedja. Thirty years later, Horwedja's father Wennefer sold the land to the master of the mystery Sen son of Iufau. The rest of the field's history is described in a papyrus from 556 BCE that is now kept in Paris as P. Louvre E 10935.

The papyrus deals with a donation of part of this land to finance a mortuary cult for an unknown person. This donation included the transfer of the former title deeds of the past owners, who are all carefully recorded in the contract. This transfer was probably symbolic, because the donor kept the other half of his land and therefore needed the title deeds himself. The donor appears to be a brother of the previous seller Wennefer, who turns out to have bought it in 557 BCE from the new owner Sen. Could this in fact be an uncle of 'our' Horwedja and did he actually buy back the family property to donate it afterward? Did the field serve as security for a loan? It is conceivable that Horwedja's father Wennefer borrowed money from Sen and as security gave him a preliminary contract for the sale of the land in question. It is clear in any case that Horwedja was not just a humble clerk in the granary office of Amun; he came from a landed family.

His colleague Neswennefer son of Sobekemhat of the granary of Amun in the district of Coptos—fellow witness in P. Louvre E 7834, 7835, and 7838, the tax receipts from the archive of Djekhy & Son—is also a witness in the land donation described in P. Louvre E 10935. Did he do so as an administrator of the Domain of Amun or was he in fact a close friend of Horwedja? We do not know, but it is conceivable at least that the ties between the two scribes may have been more than purely professional.

The Scribe of the Mat

In Egyptology, the fact that we know everything about some small detail is often the result of coincidence. In the case of the scribe of the mat we are in luck: this title was very thoroughly researched in 2000 by the Dutch Egyptologist Ben Haring in an article called "The Scribe of the Mat: From Agrarian Administration to Local Justice," published in the *Festschrift* for Jac. J. ('Jack') Janssen, the world-famous Deir al-Medina specialist.

Haring showed that the title of 'scribe of the mat' first occurs on Stela Leiden V 3 from year 33 of Sesostris I (1971–1926 BCE). This official was concerned with agriculture—or fields, harvest, and taxes, to be more precise. Other sources, for instance from the New Kingdom, indicate that the scribe of the mat also worked in legal courts, although it is not always clear whether he worked as a court scribe or made an official protocol for someone from the administration. In Deir al-Medina we regularly come across scribes of the mat as intermediaries between the vizier and the ordinary workmen. As we saw earlier, by the end of the reign of Ramesses III the workmen's wages were increasingly paid late. The twenty-ninth regnal year of Ramesses III became infamous in this respect, resulting in a letter to the vizier Ta (see above, "A Five-thousand-year Tradition"). More than once the scribes of the mat became involved in the payment of wages long overdue.

According to Haring the title 'scribe of the mat' disappeared in the Saite Period, to be replaced by 'chief scribe of the mat.' This title is last seen in P. Brooklyn 47.218.3, the famous Saite Oracle Papyrus from regnal year 14 of Psamtik I (664–610 BCE). It is believed to have fallen out of fashion in the course of the administrative reforms in the Saite Period. If, however, we look at the title of the scribe Petemestu who wrote the early demotic tax receipts P. Louvre E 7834, 7835, 7838, and 7842, it seems one cannot escape reading his title as 'scribe of the mat,' even though Erichsen and subsequent demotists read it as *sesh* 'scribe,' ignoring the mat sign. Apparently this title did not disappear under Psamtik I, but remained in use for many years afterward. It is also possible that Petemestu simply reappropriated the title, much as the choachyte Pakhorkhonsu from Saite-Period Thebes called himself Servant of the Place of Truth, a New-Kingdom title from Deir al-Medina (P. Louvre E 7847). The Saite Period in Egypt was something of a renaissance. People of the time traveled and marveled at the monuments of the past and—perhaps out of nostalgia for Egypt's old glory, perhaps from a sense of its new place in a tumultuous world— attempted in various ways to revive elements of their ancient culture.

7

Trust
Iturech 542–535 BCE

The Theban Choachytes' Association

January 542–July 538 BCE (Papyrus Louvre E 7840)

The Theban choachytes were all members of a local association. P. Louvre E 7840 is the oldest evidence that such associations existed. There also exist later demotic papyri dealing with similar clubs, among which one of the most famous is P. Berlin 3115, written between 109 and 106 BCE to record important decisions made by the Theban choachytes in the second century BCE.

On 26 April 109 BCE, during the reign of Cleopatra III and Ptolemy IX Soter, eighteen Theban choachytes met, probably in Djeme. They called themselves the choachytes of the necropolis of Djeme, which was the village built in the mortuary temple of Ramesses III, Medinet Habu. During this meeting they decided to establish a choachytes' association dedicated to the god Amenophis, the deified pharaoh Amunhotep I (reigned 1525–1504 BCE) who had become the patron saint of the necropolis. They started the day by laying down Articles of Association and Rules of Procedure, which are recorded in P. Berlin 3115.

It is interesting to note that this papyrus was once sealed with three clay seals bearing the inscription "the Royal Scribe Amunhotep." This was none other than the scribe Amunhotep son of Hapu, who was also deified. Curiously, the Theban choachytes from the sixth century BCE—the association that counted Djekhy & Son among its members—had chosen the same Amunhotep son of Hapu to be their patron saint. Modern publications have so far avoided asking whether the god Amenophis to whom Theban choachytes dedicated themselves in the second century is actually the same as the deified scribe Amunhotep whom their predecessors chose as patron saint four centuries earlier. It is not an outrageous suggestion, given that in the Ptolemaic Period Amunhotep son of Hapu became the leading healing deity in Thebes, although by this time he was actually known as Amenothes, not Amenophis. His sanctuary on the second terrace of the great temple of Queen Hatshepsut attracted pilgrims from all over Egypt, including Greeks and Romans.

One of the first things the Theban choachytes arranged on this day in April 109 BCE was their holidays. The ancient Egyptians referred to a holiday as *heru en sewer*, 'day of drinking.' Each first day of the ten-day week was set aside as a drinking day. At the same time, however, there was a strict rule that on these drinking days no more than two jugs of wine were to be consumed. Perhaps this was wisdom gained through experience.

The Theban choachytes also created a variety of rules for their new association. Swearing at the director, for instance, would cost an ordinary member five deben (455 grams). And if the director swore at an ordinary member, he would be fined ten deben (almost a kilogram). The papyrus does not state whether this was to be paid in silver, but we do know that such extreme fines in silver did exist. A variety of social situations were regulated, for instance by arranging that choachytes would attend each other's embalming ritual or funeral. As noted above, the sons of choachytes were allowed to attend the meetings from the age of ten. Once they reached sixteen, they were expected to enroll as members in their own right or risk exclusion: "Any choachyte who reaches the age of sixteen and does not come to the association of Amenophis, one will not eat nor drink with him or with someone from his household."

So there was slight social pressure to become a choachyte. The choachytes preferred to marry among themselves, and over the course of centuries they became one big family. It is also true, however, that this could be a lucrative business. In the late second century BCE the Theban choachytes managed hundreds of mummies; they might even be said to own them, because the rights to the income from these mummies could be sold, leased, inherited, and so on.

One of the tombs in which the Theban choachytes actually worked and kept their mummies can still be visited on the west bank of the Nile. In their day—2,100 years ago, in the late Hellenistic Period—this tomb was called Θυναβουνουν (Thunabunun). Now it is referred to as tomb 157 in Dra' Abu al-Naga. Θυναβουνουν is the Greek rendering of Egyptian *ta hut en Nebwenen*, 'the tomb of Nebwenen.' In fact the former owner had been a high official called Nebwenenef. He became first prophet of Amun in Thebes in the first regnal year of Ramesses II, the most powerful priest of Amun in Egypt. Like Amunhotep son of Hapu, Nebwenenef had been one of the very few commoners in ancient Egypt allowed to build his own mortuary temple in the Theban necropolis. His spacious tomb was a convenient spot for storing a large number of mummies.

P. Berlin 3115 is the latest known example of Articles of Association and Rules of Procedure from ancient Egypt. The best introduction to these texts is a book called *Les associations religieuses en Égypte d'après les documents démotiques* (1972) by the French demotist Françoise de Cenival. She was the first to collect all the texts made for these ancient professional associations, including P. Berlin 3115C: "Anyone who breaks these rules must give two talents to Pharaoh and two talents to Djeme. And he will be sued to make sure he will comply with what has been written above."

Strict rules indeed, but there were stricter. The Rules of Procedure of a professional association elsewhere in Egypt, as recorded in P. Cairo CG 31178 from 179 BCE, threatened the following in case of non-compliance:

> The one to whom it is said: "You will be the representative of our association," and he does not do this, his fine will be ten deben of silver and we will continue to have a claim on him, namely that in spite of this he shall still be the representative of the association.

The Theban choachytes from the sixth century BCE probably worked with similar rules and regulations. They also held regular networking events, meetings to end quarrels, and sometimes they met just to celebrate someone's birthday, including that of their patron deity Amunhotep son of Hapu.

There were also choachytes in Memphis in the north, a long distance from Thebes. There are quite a few key differences between the two groups. The languages spoken in Memphis and Thebes were different, as was the demotic script used during the Ptolemaic Period: Memphite demotic often looks monumental compared to the cramped Theban demotic. The contracts written in Memphis dealing with the income from mummies are often much longer than their Theban counterparts.

And specific to the Memphite necropolis was the so-called *ka* tomb, most likely a tomb hacked out of the local mountain, deep underground; there were never any tombs called *ka* tombs in Thebes.

The Memphite choachytes have, apart from a few scattered publications, so far been neglected in the scientific literature. The best introduction is a chapter in the book *Memphis under the Ptolemies* (1988) by the British papyrologist Dorothy Thompson. Worldwide there are probably only five Egyptologists studying the Memphite choachytes. The latest milestone was set by the British demotist Cary Martin, who in 2009 published (and partly republished) the Memphite demotic collection kept in Leiden, including a papyrus from St. Petersburg and one from London: *Demotic Papyri from the Memphite Necropolis: In the Collections of the National Museum of Antiquities in Leiden, the British Museum and the Hermitage Museum*. It is a fertile area for new research that could contribute significantly to our knowledge of ancient Egypt. The papyri from Leiden had been waiting for an integral publication for 180 years, and there are plenty of papyri in many, many museums still awaiting scientific publication.

The archive of Djekhy & Son contains one papyrus dealing with the local choachytes' association of which Iturech was a member, together with his brother Khausenmin and his uncle Rery. Djekhy himself is not mentioned in the association's records. P. Louvre E 7840 measures twenty-six by fifty-eight centimeters—which is rather large for a documentary papyrus—and it contains some of the records of the Theban choachytes' association between 542 and 538 BCE. The fact that it was found together with the personal papers of Iturech once again indicates that the people from Djekhy & Son were influential among the Theban choachytes. It is conceivable that Iturech asked if he could take the papyrus home, because it records what was probably a key moment in his life, as we will soon see.

At first glance this papyrus—containing thirteen columns spread along the front and back (two were erased by the scribe) and two small marginal notes apparently scribbled in wherever the scribe felt like putting them—does not look very attractive. Most of the text consists of dates and lists of names, often followed by numbers or amounts.

Twenty-five centuries later it is not easy to understand the document's exact purpose, but the reasons for recording some dates and meetings are fairly clear. Favorite dates were the first month of the akhet season and the third month of the peret season. While the precise day of a meeting is never mentioned, we know that the Egyptian new year started with the first month of akhet; it would make sense to hold a meeting then. P. Louvre E 7840 contains some of the notes taken at these new year's meetings, for instance:

> Regnal year 29, first month of the akhet season under Pharaoh l.p.h. Amasis l.p.h.
> This silver of the income—specification:
> Petemin son of Nesmin: 4¼ kite silver.
> Petosiris son of Iturech: 3⅓ kite silver.
> Neshorpakhrat son of Petehorresne: 2½ kite silver.
> Peteamunip son of Hor for . . . : 2⅓ ¹⁄₁₂ kite silver.
> Ankhhor son of Hor for taking the *men* vase: 2½ kite silver.
> Anyuuchay son of Iturech for service: ⅔ ¹⁄₁₂ kite silver.
> Khausenmut son of Amunhotepiu for service: ⅔ ¹⁄₁₂ kite silver.
> Rery son of Heryrem for listening: ⅔ kite silver.
> Peteamunip son of Ituru for questioning: ⅔ kite silver.

At first glance this is not a highly informative text, except for the fact that it records what took place at the annual new year's meeting of the Theban choachytes' association. Apparently this event also served to close the books of the fiscal year 28. Looked at in the context of the archive of Djekhy & Son, however, we can actually learn more about this note made in January 542 BCE.

The heading shows that this is a list of the income of the association, about 160 grams of silver, one kite being the tenth of the approximately ninety-one-gram deben. Recall that Djekhy quarreled with a choachyte called Petosiris son of Iturech (here mentioned in line 4) in 559 BCE about the rights to service the mummies in a specific tomb (P. Louvre E 7848). In the end Djekhy and his business partners had won the case, and Djekhy had continued to do business with Petosiris, for instance leasing land together (P. BM EA 10432). Is the Petosiris son of Iturech mentioned here in line 4 the same man Djekhy quarreled with and leased a field with? Or is it his grandson, named after him?

We also know that Neshorpakhrat son of Petehorresne (line 5) would eventually become the new overseer of the necropolis. He is the author of two contracts in the archive of Djekhy & Son: P. Louvre E 7836 and 7839. In this meeting record, however, he is still listed without any title and elsewhere in P. Louvre E 7840 he is referred to as "the son" of the overseer of the necropolis. This suggests that he had not yet stepped into the role of overseer. It is only in a small note in column IIA that he is called overseer of the necropolis for the first time.

We know from another notation that Rery son of Heryrem (line 10) was the elder brother of a boy who years later would marry a female choachyte, Mrs. Tsenhor. Just like Djekhy & Son, she left an archive that has contributed much to our knowledge of Egypt in the Late Period. This archive was published in 1994 in a brilliant book called *Les papyrus démotiques de Tsenhor: Les archives privées d'une femme égyptienne du temps de Darius Ier*, by the Dutch demotist and legal historian Pieter Willem Pestman. Maybe, just maybe, this boy—if he had reached the age of ten by the time this document was written—was present at this new year's meeting in 542 BCE, making this tiny note special after all.

These men knew each other well. They had had their quarrels, but who knew whether they would still be present next year? Today the quarrels were set aside. Today was a day of celebration, for the new year had started.

By far the most intriguing name is that of Anyuuchay son of Iturech. We know that at one point in time he managed the finances of the choachytes' association. In the third month of the peret season, one day between 5 July and 4 August 542 BCE, he received a large sum on behalf of the choachytes' association. The tasks of the chief financial officer of an ancient Egyptian religious association were clearly defined: He received and recorded all membership fees, fines, debts, arrears, and securities. He gave financial support to the other members of the association, for instance if there was a death in the family or if a member was wrongfully sued. He also determined the best way to use the association's assets. Although we know much about the role of Anyuuchay son of Iturech, we do not know whether he was a son of 'our' choachyte Iturech. Given the prominent position of the family of Djekhy & Son, this is a tempting inference. One is even led to wonder whether Djekhy and Iturech had once held the same position; if this were the case, it might help to explain why people asked them to act as trustees.

What kind of income was reported during this new year's meeting? The "taking of the *men* vase" (line 7) by the choachyte Ankhhor refers to a religious rite. In the temple of Dendara, downstream to the north of Thebes, a festival was held in the same new year's month—from the eighteenth to the twenty-second day of the first month of the akhet season to be precise—to celebrate the return of the goddess Hathor from Nubia. On the third day of this festival a hymn would be sung for this same *men* vase, which would then be offered to Hathor. We can assume that on this day—also known as the Festival of Drunkenness—people not only sang, but also drank quite a lot.

It does not seem very likely that Ankhhor was planning to visit the Dendara festival on behalf of the Theban choachytes' association. The Festival of Drunkenness was, in fact, also a Theban carnival that involved the entire population. In 2006 the American archaeologist Betsy Bryan found evidence of this festival at the temple of Mut, which would have been very close to where Djekhy & Son lived. It is believed that these festivals were attended by tens of thousands of people—Herodotus records seven hundred thousand—possibly near the Porch of Drunkenness built there by Queen Hatshepsut. In this context, and since Hathor is associated with merriment, dance, love, and sex, it is not surprising that the Rules of Procedure of the Theban choachytes from the second century BCE—the same P. Berlin 3115 described at the beginning of this chapter—contained strict regulations when it came to drinking alcohol during meetings, to prevent things getting out of hand. As for the reference to Ankhhor and the 'taking of the *men* vase,' does this mean he had attended the last year's festival and made some money there which he now handed over to the association?

Looking again at P. Louvre E 7840, the short entries on 'listening' (line 10) and 'questioning' (line 11)—the latter by the choachyte Peteamunip son of Ituru, a former business partner of Djekhy in 556 BCE and apparently still active in the local choachytes' association—suggest that there had been a conflict between some members of the association. We know that Djekhy regularly quarreled with his colleagues (P. Louvre E 7861, 7848, and 7847). The Theban choachytes preferred to handle their own affairs behind closed doors, without outside interference. A hearing would be held during which a committee of prominent members would question the choachytes involved and listen to what they had to say.

The Patron Saint

The third month of the peret season was the second important month in the lives of the Theban choachytes; we can infer this from the fact that twice the scribe of P. Louvre E 7840 devoted a whole column to a meeting during this period. Again, he merely listed names and numbers or amounts. One

of these meetings took place in 538 BCE, with eighteen members present; it is possible that more people were there than the scribe recorded,
for instance if each choachyte had brought a son who was not a member
of the association. It is likely that on this day the Theban choachytes
celebrated the birthday of their patron saint Amunhotep son of Hapu,
the deified scribe from the reign of King Amunhotep III (reigned c.
1391–1353 BCE). He was revered as a god well into the Ptolemaic Period,
attracting pilgrims from all over Egypt, but mostly locals imploring him
to heal their ailments, including infertility.

The demotic text below, possibly dated to 219 BCE, was written on a
wooden writing board discovered by the French demotist Michel Malinine in the shop of the famous collector George Michaélides in Cairo in
1954. It is a prayer by a priest of Amun who desperately wants a woman
(probably his wife) to become pregnant. The writing board was probably
placed in or near the shrine of Amunhotep for maximum effect:

> With the voice of a servant. The god's father and priest of Amun-Ra
> King of Gods Wesirweris son of Hor addresses his lord, the royal
> scribe Amunhotep son of Hapu, the great god: "If it so happens that
> Taype daughter of Petemestu becomes pregnant, I will give one
> more deben of silver—that is five stater in silver—and that is one
> deben of silver again, makes a total of two deben of silver for the
> work (?), on the day I am told to do this. My great lord, if only he
> would celebrate millions of jubilee festivals! This good scribe! I am
> your servant and son of your servant from the beginning (of times).
> Do not forget Wesirweris son of Hor son of Wesirweris! From the
> beginning of times (. . .)." Written in regnal year 3, third month of
> the peret season, day 23 (?).

In ancient Egypt, the prayer business was a flourishing industry and people were very resourceful when it came to attracting the attention of the
deity most suitable for the occasion. A British archaeological team has
been active in Saqqara—ancient Memphis—for many years now and has
unearthed countless demotic ostraca and papyri. Many of these have been
published in recent years, including some of the most difficult.

A few years ago the British demotist John Ray—probably one of the
best scholars in this field—published a small demotic text written on a
piece of linen. It was found by the team of the Egypt Exploration Society

in the season of 1968–69 in what is now referred to as the Main Temple Enclosure. The text—for the time being labeled Saqqara H5-1660 [3545]—probably dates back to the Thirtieth Dynasty or slightly later (from about 380 BCE onward). It had originally been fixed to some twigs to maintain its shape, but it had been badly crushed for centuries, so the excavators had to relax and press it for quite some time before they could begin to interpret it, constantly readjusting the fibers to keep the text legible. Because of this, even the dimensions are only approximate, thirty by twenty centimeters. Reading demotic is difficult, but reading demotic on a linen surface borders on the insane, prompting Ray's remark in the *Journal of Egyptian Archaeology* 91 (2005):

> The purpose of this was no doubt to enable the text to be inserted into the mud-brick wall of a shrine or chapel, or into the frame of a gate or door, so that the text would face inwards towards the shrine, where it could be read by the god Osirapis as it fluttered in the breeze. However, given the difficulty of the hand on such an unsteady medium, the god can be forgiven if he chose to wait for a still day. The writer was presumably confident that Osirapis would be able to decipher this plea, and we have no reason to disparage his hopes, even if our modern-day ability to read this text is a long way short of supernatural.

John Ray's efforts with this difficult text have produced a preliminary translation that will no doubt occupy the minds of Egyptologists for decades to come. The gist of Saqqara H5-1660 [3545] is:

> With the servant's voice. Wennefer (?) son of Chayayn (?) prays to my great Osirapis: Irpy, the daughter of Petosiris, has taken away my woman and complained against me (?). I have no protection except Osirapis, so do justice to her which is severe (?). Do not hesitate with her and look upon my heart. Tough will be the . . . heart that you must show to her. Let them speak to every man about the fierce (?) retribution (?), the way you will deal with her. Do justice (?) for us (?). I beg (?) [this]. It is written.

Let us return to Djekhy & Son. The notes made by the scribe of P. Louvre E 7840 during the meeting of the Theban choachytes' organization in the third month of peret in 538 BCE clearly suggest that Iturech was a prominent member: he is mentioned third in the list of eighteen names, and whereas the other members received ten measures of resin, Iturech received twenty. This was a day of celebration. Twenty jars of beer were drunk, thirteen having been brought in. This combination of beer and moringa oil, a measure of which was also given to each member present that day, is also known from a New Kingdom papyrus written 650 years before Iturech was born (P. Anastasi III). This papyrus describes how sweet moringa was placed on the heads of young men who were celebrating. We can now imagine these eighteen Theban choachytes sitting in their headquarters or perhaps a tent specially erected for the occasion on a day between 4 July and 3 August—it would be stiflingly hot outside—together with a statue of Amunhotep son of Hapu, smelling of beer and moringa and exchanging all kinds of news and bad jokes, to return home at the end of the day in a rather festive mood.

It is clear that although P. Louvre E 7840 at first sight appears to be a rather boring collection of lists, it is in fact a rich source of information if examined in the context of the archive of Djekhy & Son. The papyrus forms just a small part of the records kept by the choachytes' association, however, not even fully covering the years 542–538 BCE. And relevant data seem to be missing. For instance, what appears to be a membership list for 541 BCE does not mention Iturech, although we know from other passages that he was still part of the association: one passage tells us that in 541 he swore an oath before the patron saint; in a list of twenty members between 544 and 542, he appears second; and—as we saw above—he took part in the celebration of the anniversary of Amunhotep son of Hapu in 538. Maybe he was ill on that day in 541, or the list was incomplete, or it actually served another purpose.

The oath Iturech swore in 541 BCE appears to have been important, and the event was duly recorded by the association's scribe. It may be that this oath was the very reason why P. Louvre E 7840 is found in the archive of Djekhy & Son. It is probable that he took this oath in the presence of his colleagues during the celebration of a new year. This passage also illustrates some of the intricacies connected with reading early demotic sources:

May he (Amunhotep son of Hapu) grant a good year to the overseer of the troop, the lesonis (chief financial officer), the scribe, <and> Iturech and the people doing service before the face of Amunhotep: Iturech and Hor son of Paybes. Neshorpakhrat, the overseer of the necropolis, has caused that an oath is taken behind (?) you, Amunhotep, together with Iturech son of Djekhy, until eternity.

The name Iturech is mentioned three times in this short note, but only in the last mention can we be certain that this is 'our' choachyte Iturech. Moreover, since the ancient Egyptians did not use commas, we don't even know whether the first reference should be read 'the scribe Iturech' or 'the scribe and Iturech.' Although the name Iturech is written on a new line, which is suggestive of the second reading, we cannot rely on this interpretation since the whole note consists of very short lines; the line break may have been due to space constraints. But apparently the overseer of the necropolis Neshorpakhrat had arranged for Iturech to take an oath in the presence of the patron saint Amunhotep son of Hapu. We do not know whether the Theban choachytes had their own headquarters, but if they had (it is not unlikely), there are various possible locations for it. It could of course have been a tent erected for the occasion, and in that case the choachytes may have brought their own statue of Amunhotep son of Hapu along for the celebration of the new year. The temple of Amun in Karnak itself is another possibility. A number of giant granite statues of Amunhotep son of Hapu have been found there and any of these could have been the statue addressed by Iturech. A third alternative was a tomb at Gurnet Murai, found by the Italian archaeologist Dino Bidoli in the 1960s. He claimed that this was Amunhotep's tomb, but the actual tomb has not been found to this day. The tomb found by Bidoli was referred to by the locals as Bab al-Hagar, 'The door of the (loose) stones,' an accurate description of the state in which it was found. But this was a tomb of poor quality, not fitting for a man like Amunhotep son of Hapu, who was allowed by Amunhotep III to build his own mortuary temple between the royal mortuary temples on the Theban west bank. This temple near Medinet Habu would be another possible location for a new year's meeting of the Theban choachytes.

During the Ptolemaic Period, however, the most famous sanctuary of Amunhotep son of Hapu was at the mortuary temple of Queen Hatshepsut at Deir al-Bahari adjacent to the Assasif, the most famous location of tombs of high-ranking Saite dignitaries. This was a place where the Theban choachytes worked on a regular basis—Iturech, for instance, provided his services to a member of the Besmut family buried in a tomb in the Hatshepsut complex. Given its reputation, Deir al-Bahari would seem to be the ideal place for the choachytes to gather to celebrate the new year. The Polish excavation reports, however, do not mention a Saite predecessor to the Ptolemaic Amunhotep sanctuary excavated there in the 1980s. It is possible that the Ptolemaic sanctuary was built in that location because it was already sacred—possibly since at least the Saite Period.

The actual cult of Amunhotep son of Hapu at Deir al-Bahari went on well into the second century CE. The Bark Shrine at Hatshepsut's complex and the two chambers behind it are believed to comprise a likely location for the cult due to the absence of graffiti, which suggests this space was not accessible to the public. Various inscriptions from the late third and early fourth centuries CE left by an association of iron workers from Hermonthis—a town nearby—show that these men held ritual banquets there, drinking beer in honor of a god that may have been Amunhotep son of Hapu. It would be a strong parallel to the meetings of the Theban choachytes mentioned in P. Louvre E 7840.

The healing role of Amunhotep also continued well into the Christian era. Around 600 CE a monastery was built at the spot of his former temple, promising medical treatment—or rather miracles—to true believers. In the adjacent area of Sheikh Abd al-Qurna the local saint is still visited by women with fertility problems to this day.

Earlier it was seen that business conflicts between the Theban choachytes could be settled by taking an oath before the lunar deity Khonsuemwasneferhotep on the fifteenth day of the lunar month (when there was a full moon). The oath in P. Louvre E 7840 was probably of a different nature. It was taken by Iturech during the celebration of the new year. Even if we are able to exclude the possibility that this oath was the result of a business conflict, it would still mark some special event that was very important for the Theban choachytes' association, because it involved both the patron saint and the choachyte Iturech son of Djekhy. Was it taken because Iturech had won the Businessman of the Year Award, or had he risen to some prominent position in the organization? Is it relevant that he took the oath behind—a reading problem, by the way—instead of before the god? We will never know. What we do know is that P. Louvre E 7840 was kept in the archive of Djekhy & Son, to be sold 2,500 years later to August Eisenlohr by Muhammad Muhassib.

Egyptian New Year

The Egyptians had a number of calendars—at least a civil calendar and a lunisolar calendar—counting 365 days, which was a quarter of a day short. This caused some problems, because the seasons and dates of the civil calendar slowly started to diverge, only to coincide again after 1,260 years. Eloquent proof of the problems that arose from the diverging calendars used in ancient Egypt appears in P. Anastasi IV 10.1–2 from the New Kingdom: "Come and rescue me, Amun! Rescue me in this horrible year. The state of the sun is such that it does not rise. The peret season has ended up in the shemu season, the months are wrong, and the hours are jumbled up."

There were also different new year's days, for instance in the temples where local mythology played a prominent part. Civil new year fell on the first day of the akhet season. A year would last 360 days and be followed by five liminal days on which people were advised to keep a low profile. These were the days when the lion goddess Sakhmet was particularly powerful, supported by all kinds of awful demons intent on annihilating mankind. Even if in Deir al-Medina the workmen did not work in the royal tomb on these five days, the delivery of foodstuffs and other commodities to the village continued as usual. Often in the night before new year a lamp or torch would be lit to ward off evil spirits, a custom still seen in many parts of the world today.

At times like these the Egyptian priests in the temples were very active, because the temples were believed to play a key role in keeping the cosmic balance—ma'at—in order. High-ranking officials would present gifts to the king to celebrate the coming year. In Deir al-Medina the people sometimes used these extra days to bring water offerings to the dead or to enjoy a meal at night inside their tomb chapels, which were next to the village. The best-known new year's objects from the Saite Period —the age of Djekhy & Son—are the bottles presented to the living and the dead, flattened jugs with a narrow neck often flanked by baboons. These were the sacred animals of the baboon god Thoth (Djehuty), and this was his day. The bottleneck sometimes also bears a formula wishing the receiver of the bottle well. We do not know what these new year's bottles contained, but it is likely to have been water, oil, or some kind of ointment. One can easily imagine the choachytes exchanging these bottles filled with moringa oil to celebrate the new year.

A Complicated Deal

September 535 BCE (Papyrus Louvre E 7833 and 7837)

P. Louvre E 7833 and 7837 have had Egyptologists scratching their heads ever since they became known. These are two different land lease contracts written by two different scribes between 1 September and 1 October 535 BCE. To add to our confusion they are also known under the ghost numbers P. Louvre E 7833A and 7833B. In both contracts the landlord is the priest of Amun Wedjahor son of Dyamunawykhonsu (his brother Rery and his own son Imuthes are also mentioned). The fields he leased out were in the Domain of Amun in the district of Coptos in the high land The Stable of the Milk Can of Amun, the same spot where Iturech worked his own fields.

Wedjahor is known from another papyrus in the British Museum, P. BM EA 10117, which probably dates from 542 BCE. P. BM EA 10117 is a sale of land bordered by a plot managed or perhaps owned by Wedjahor: "Its north: the fields of the god's father of Amun Wedjahor son of Dyamunawykhonsu that were given to the wet nurse of Pharaoh l.p.h. NN."

This concise description offers another good example of the difficulties encountered when interpreting ancient Egyptian (legal) texts. The scribe's intention is unclear. Were these fields given to Wedjahor so he could maintain the funerary cult of the royal wet nurse? Or were they given to the wet nurse by the Domain of Amun, which Wedjahor managed? Finding the answer to this is not easy.

The same difficulty occurs in P. Louvre E 7833 and 7837. Although Wedjahor refers to the fields he is renting as "my fields," this does not necessarily prove that he owned them. They too may have belonged to the Domain of Amun. Both contracts are with the same lessee: the cattle keeper of Montu Petemontu son of Pawakhamun, an old acquaintance of the choachyte Iturech. In P. Louvre E 7833 he is mentioned alone (maybe representing a group of business partners), while in P. Louvre E 7837 other business associates are explicitly mentioned, although not by name.

Iturech is not mentioned in either contract. They probably ended up in the archive of Djekhy & Son because Iturech and Petemontu had done business together before (see above, "More Than Ten Hectares of Land?"), and Petemontu trusted his old business partner. Alternatively, Iturech may have been directly involved in the land leases as an anonymous business partner.

—w—

What makes P. Louvre E 7833 and 7837 so special? To start with, the two papyri have been mixed up in the literature from time to time, which has led to some analytical confusion. Some Egyptologists have even suggested that one contract was written to replace the other.

The Austrian legal historian Erwin Seidl—not a man to include things lightly in his epoch-making *Ägyptische Rechtsgeschichte der Saiten- und Perserzeit* (1968)—thought P. Louvre E 7837 had been the original contract. This contained a clause stating that Petemontu and his business partners would supply five plowing oxen and the landlord Wedjahor would supply the sixth. The harvest was to be divided as follows: before subtraction of taxes and other costs, Petemontu would receive 55.6 percent of the harvest and Wedjahor 44.4 percent. Seidl suggests that Petemontu soon found he could not supply five oxen, so that a new contract had to be made (P. Louvre E 7833), wherein Wedjahor agreed supply two oxen instead of the original one.

However, George Hughes had already undermined Seidl's hypothesis years before. In his unsurpassed *Saite Demotic Land Leases* (1952), which included some of the texts from the archive of Djekhy & Son, Hughes argued persuasively that these were two different contracts. The different contract terms (on the one hand, one lessee and two oxen; on the other, a group of lessees and six oxen) were sufficient, he said, to establish that these texts referred to different plots of land.

A number of other arguments support Hughes's point. First, Petemontu was a cattle keeper; it is unlikely that he would have had difficulty obtaining the required five oxen. Second, the so-called replacement contract P. Louvre E 7833 offers significantly less generous terms for the lessee Petemontu. It would have been better for the landlord to insist that the alleged original contract, P. Louvre E 7837 (more favorable to the lessee), be made invalid on the spot, for instance by striking through the text—there are examples of this—or simply by tearing up the papyrus, but he did neither. This in itself, coupled with the fact that both papyri were officially signed by witnesses and kept side by side in the archive of Djekhy & Iturech, is the best argument in support of these being two independent contracts, and that Petemontu leased two different plots of land from Wedjahor in 535 BCE.

It is not known why these two land leases were written by two different scribes. It may be as simple as that they were written on different days, and in different offices. The fact that the contracts had different witnesses supports this interpretation. A parallel translation of the two contracts is offered in Table 6 to facilitate comparison, and to highlight why interpreting these texts has proved so difficult.

Table 6. Parallel translation of two land lease contracts

P. Louvre E 7833	P. Louvre E 7837
Regnal year 36, first month of the shemu season under Pharaoh l.p.h. Amasis l.p.h. The god's father Wedjahor son of Dyamunawykhonsu has said to the cattle keeper of the Domain of Montu Lord of Thebes, Petemontu son of Pawakhamun, whose mother is Ruru:	Regnal year 36, first month of the shemu season under Pharaoh l.p.h. Amasis l.p.h. The god's father Wedjahor son of Dyamunawykhonsu has said to the cattle keeper of the Domain of Montu Lord of Thebes, Petemontu son of Pawakhamun, whose mother is Ruru:
"I have made available to you this yoke of plowing oxen to plow with them in the name of the god's father Rery son of Dyamunawykhonsu, you being with it as the cultivator on each of the fields of mine that you will till, which are in the Domain of Amun in the district of Coptos in the west of the high land The Stable of the Milk Can of Amun from regnal year 36 to regnal year 37."	"I have leased to you my fields which are in the Domain of Amun in the district of Coptos in the west of the high land The Stable of the Milk Can of Amun to cultivate them from regnal year 36 to regnal year 37 with these three yokes of plowing oxen, makes six oxen. Specification: you and your business partners five oxen and I one ox to complete (the specification), you being the person who will put my ox to work."
"When harvest has occurred in regnal year 37, I will take 33.3 percent of all grain and shoots that have come up on the fields that you will till with the abovementioned yoke of oxen, about which you have drawn up (a document) to the name of Rery son of Dyamunawykhonsu, my brother, with respect to the harvest of the field."	"When harvest has occurred in regnal year 37, I will take 33.3 percent of all grain and shoots that have come up in the name of my share of owner of the field, and we will divide the remainder in six parts. Specification: to you and your business partners five shares and to me because of my ox one share to complete (the specification). You are liable for the loss due to mismanagement by the cultivator, whereas I will pay the harvest tax of the Domain of Amun from the 33.3 percent of the abovementioned share of the owner of the field."

P. Louvre E 7833	P. Louvre E 7837
"I will ensure that the scribes of the Domain of Amun will be far from you regarding their harvest tax of the Domain of Amun, whereas I will not be able to send a scribe of the Kalasirians (police) before you in the name of their harvest tax of the Domain of Amun."	"I will ensure that the scribes of the Domain of Amun will be far from you regarding their harvest tax."
"We will divide the remainder in four shares among ourselves. Specification: to me three shares because of this yoke of plowing oxen and the seedcorn in the name of the god's father Rey son of Dyamunawykhonsu, and to you one share for the tilling, cultivation, and all its cultivator shall do from regnal year 36 to regnal year 37 to complete (the specification)."	
"The scribes of the Domain of Amun will measure my fields in my name, whereas I will take the loss due to mismanagement by the cultivator that I will find on the abovementioned fields, on top of the shares of the god's father Rery son of Dyamunawykhonsu, and (will do this) from your share, it being of good quality. You are liable for the mismanagement by the cultivator of this yoke of oxen. Profit and loss will be shared between us, as two business partners."	"The scribes of the Domain of Amun will measure my fields in my name. If I withdraw to prevent you from cultivating my fields from regnal year 36 to regnal year 37 and in accordance with the abovementioned clauses, I will give you one (deben of) silver (from the) Treasury of Thebes, without citing any document."
In the writing of Djedmutiufankh son of Inaros.	In the writing of Teos son of the god's father of Amun Ipy.

As already noted, most land leases in Egypt in the sixth century BCE were oral contracts. They were legally binding and governed by customary law, some sense of which we can glean from P. Mattha.[1] But for complicated transactions, written leases were preferred. A side-by-side comparison of the specific terms of P. Louvre E 7833 and 7837 (Table 7) shows how complicated the payment and breach clauses actually are, explaining why these leases were made in writing.

Table 7. Comparison of P. Louvre E 7833 and P. Louvre E 7837

Party	Receives	Pays
Landlord: Wedjahor	P. Louvre E 7833 33.3 percent of the harvest and ¾ x ⅔ = 50 percent because of a contribution by landlord's brother	Harvest tax of the Domain of Amun = 10 percent of the total harvest
Lessee: Petemontu	P. Louvre E 7833 ¼ x ⅔ = 16.7 percent for cultivation	The loss due to mismanagement (including the oxen) by the cultivator
Landlord: Wedjahor	P. Louvre E 7837 33.3 percent of the harvest and ⅙ x ⅔ = 11.1 percent of the harvest for his plowing ox	Harvest tax of the Domain of Amun = 10 percent of the total harvest, and a fine of one deben of silver if he does not live up to the agreement
Lessees: Petemontu and business partners	P. Louvre E 7837 ⅚ x ⅔ = 55.6 percent of the harvest for their oxen and cultivation	The loss due to mismanagement by the cultivator

8

People
Iturech 539 BCE

Iturech Buys a Son

March–April 539 BCE (Papyrus Louvre E 7832)

One day in the spring of 539 BCE—between 6 March and 5 April—Iturech and a man called Hor son of Petiese and Mrs. Tayuau met, probably at the office of the scribe Nehemsukhonsu, along with eleven witnesses.

The scribe Nehemsukhonsu ('Khonsu has saved him') is otherwise unknown. Egyptian scribes often added their title to their signature, but he did not. It is a shame, because a title often indicates whether someone worked for a specific temple or government office. Iturech, one of the stakeholders, signed the document in person.[1] It was a special day for him: on this day Iturech bought Hor to be his son. The major part of P. Louvre E 7832 consists of the statement made by Hor:

> You (Iturech) have satisfied my heart with my silver to be your son. I am your son, together with my children who will be born to me, together with all I possess and will acquire. No one on earth will be able to exercise authority over me except you, be it father, mother, brother, sister, master, mistress, or any creditor or myself. My children are the children of your children forever. The one who will come to you, say-ing: "This is not your son," namely anyone on earth, including father, mother, brother, sister, master, mistress, or any creditor or myself, even if he will give you silver or grain that will enter your heart (i.e., satisfies you), then I will still be your son, together with my children, forever.

In short, Hor's statement means that he was satisfied with the price Itu-rech had paid, and agreed in exchange to become his son. Moreover,

133

the exchange bound not only Hor, but also his children. And it was a permanent condition: it could not be undone through any subsequent payment by a third party. Having a son was a lifelong ambition for any ancient Egyptian. A son would ensure that property remained in the family into the next generation. A son would look after his parents when they were old. A son was a pension, and also the best guarantee that the parents' mortuary cult would be maintained; this was not just a question of nostalgia, but considered vital for their well-being in the afterlife. The importance of sons—and especially the eldest son—can be seen in the legal manual P. Mattha (VIII 30, IX 7 and IX 29–30):

> Suppose that someone dies, being in the possession of a field, a garden, a house, an income from the temple, or a slave, this person also having children, but never having made a will for his children during his lifetime. In that case his eldest son will take the possessions. If the younger brothers file a complaint against their eldest brother, saying: "He should give us a share of the possessions of our father," and if the eldest brother then draws up a list of the younger brothers—the children of his father, the ones who are still alive and the ones who died before their father died, including himself—he can take for himself whatever he wants from the fields, gardens, and houses. What he wants is what should be given to him. The documents and contracts about repayment of grain or goods that belonged to his father but are now with other people, they should be returned to him, except contracts that were written through his father's initiative, because these cannot be returned to him. As far as the remainder of the possessions is concerned, these should be divided according to the number of his (the deceased father's) children. The male children may then choose their shares according to their date of birth, and subsequently his female children may choose (their shares) according to their date of birth. If it so happens that a person among them dies after their father died (but before the division of the inheritance) and has no child, the eldest brother will take possession of this share. If someone dies without having received his or her share, the eldest brother will take possession of this share. If a person dies after he (or she) has received his or her share and is without child, the eldest brother will take possession of this share.
>
> As for the man who gets daughters first and sons afterwards, the male children will produce an eldest son.

This transaction raises some serious questions, not least of which is why it took place at all. Did Iturech have no children of his own in 539 BCE? This would be strange in a country where large families were the rule. By now Iturech would have been in his thirties and a very attractive candidate for marriage, given his position among the Theban choachytes. Moreover, Hor's statement, "My children are the children of your children forever" suggests that even if Iturech did not have children yet, Hor assumed he someday would. Iturech would thus not need to buy a son for any of the traditional reasons children were considered necessary—maintaining the bloodline and the family property, and taking care of their parents, their parents' funeral, and subsequent mortuary cult. And in that case, we must look for another explanation for this unusual purchase.

One possibility is that Hor had been given as security for a loan. Recall that less than twenty years before, Djekhy had provided a loan secured by a broad range of the debtor's property, including his house, male servants, female servants, sons, daughters, silver, copper, clothing, oil, grain, or any other movable or immovable property (P. BM EA 10113). It is possible that Iturech acquired Hor as the result of a similar deal, where the debtor was unable to repay his debt. Intriguingly, P. Louvre E 7832 is unique. This contract is, in fact, an ingenious adaptation of earlier contracts in which people sell themselves as slaves to repay a debt, but in P. Louvre E 7832 the scribe replaced 'slave' with 'son.' The technical term for this kind of adaptation is *Umgehungsgeschäft*.

The famous Austrian legal historian Erwin Seidl once noted that Egyptian contracts in which debtors sell themselves as slaves disappear from the record after regnal year 8 of Amasis (563 BCE), although his observation should be treated with some caution because of the small number of papyri we have left from this period. P. Louvre E 7832 was written in regal year 32 of Amasis. It is possible that Amasis—who had a reputation as a lawmaker that was known even to Herodotus—had issued a law prohibiting the repayment of a debt by selling oneself into slavery to the creditor. Replacing 'slave' with 'son' could thus be a neat legal trick to get around this prohibition.

This is an interesting hypothesis, but we do not know if it is true, if for no other reason than that we do not know whether Amasis actually enacted such a prohibition. Buying slaves was certainly still possible, as evidenced by P. Turin 2122 from 517 BCE. Note, however, the curious echoes between the slave's statement in P. Bibliothèque Nationale 223, from the same period, and Hor's statement upon his sale to Iturech:

> Record and do all that has been said above (about the sale). My heart is satisfied with it. I am your slave, together with my children and all that belongs to us and what we will still acquire. They will never be free before you for ever and ever.

Another possible explanation is amusingly illustrated by these maxims and admonitions of P. Insinger:

P. Insinger col. VIII 20–IX 18
The tenth teaching.
The art of not failing when raising your son.
A stupid son who has not been raised (properly) by his father is like a stone statue.
For a son it is a good and blessed faith to accept a teaching without asking questions.
A teaching has had no effect if the result is a bad deed (?).
The boy who has not been spoiled because of his belly is the one who will not be reproached.
He who contains his private parts is the one whose name will not be connected with ridicule and shame.
(. . .)
The punishment of a father will not kill a son.
Whoever loves his spoiled son will go to ground with him.
Stick and shame will protect their owner from the evil spirits.
The son who has not been raised, his death will cause amazement.
The heart of his father does not desire a long life for him.
The wisest among the (other) children is the child that deserves to live.
Better the son of another than a stupid son who is cursed.
Some people have not been raised (properly), but are still able to tell others how to live.
Some people can learn, but can't live accordingly.

P. Insinger col. XII 14–22

One will not learn the heart of a man in his character if one has not
sent him out on a mission.

One will not learn the heart of a wise man if one has not tested him in
a business transaction.

One will not learn the heart of an honest man if one has not asked for
advice when the accounts are settled.

(...)

One will not learn the heart of a companion if one has not asked him
for advice in a dangerous situation.

(...)

One will not learn the heart of a son until the moment he is asked for
some property.

One will not learn the heart of a servant as long as his master is not
under attack.

One will not learn the heart of a woman, just like heaven.

It is not known how old Hor was at the time of the sale. Some Egyptologists believe that because the first witness signature on the back of the
papyrus is not Hor's but that of an adult man whom we do not know,
Hor was probably a minor needing the support of a legal guardian. The
position of a signature in the list of witnesses is sometimes indicative, and
often the top signature is that of someone with a direct interest in the
sale or contract. In P. Louvre E 7833, for instance, the landlord Wedjahor
signed at the top of the list of witnesses, immediately followed by the signature of his son Imouthes. In the land lease P. Louvre E 7837, Wedjahor
signed first, then the scribe's son, then his own son Imouthes. A curious
case is that of the witness Hor son of Besmut in abnormal hieratic P. BM
EA 10906 and 10907, which is an intricate loan involving two goatherds
called Tjaynahebu and Payuyuhor. The texts were probably written in the
seventh century BCE. In P. BM EA 10906 Hor signed at the bottom of the
list of witnesses on the back of the papyrus: "Before Hor son of Besmut,
regarding the deposition of Tjaynahebu about the document which is
above." In P. BM EA 10907 the witnesses once again signed on the back
of the papyrus, but this time Hor placed his signature at the bottom of
the front of the papyrus, immediately below the signature of the scribe:
"Before Hor son of Besmut, regarding the deposition of Payuyuhor about
the document which is above." In these cases, we do not know what Hor's

interest in the contracts was, although the placement of his signature in highly conspicuous spots and the fact that he probably came from the famous Besmut family strongly suggest that this interest existed.

We do not know what happened to Hor in later life. In 506 BCE a Hor son of Iturech is mentioned in a papyrus now in Turin—with the inventory number 2125—but we cannot be certain it was the same man; these were rather common names in Thebes.

The Dutch demotist and legal historian P.W. Pestman, who studied demotic with Michel Malinine in Paris, once related how Malinine, when it was time for lunch, simply took P. Louvre E 7832 to one of the many restaurants along the northern bank of the Seine to resume his lesson there. This, however, is a relic of the past. Today, P. Louvre E 7832 is safely kept in a large underground vault deep below the Louvre.

9

Earth
Iturech 536–534 BCE

A Cattle Keeper of Montu

October–November 536 BCE (Papyrus Louvre E 7836)
The cattle keeper of the Domain of Montu Petemontu son of Pawakhamun was a preferred supplier of Djekhy & Son. He is known from an
earlier visit to the scribes of the Domain of Amun in the district of Coptos in May 536 BCE. He was there to pay the harvest tax for the 537–536
season, together with his own brother and the owner of the land, the
choachyte Iturech son of Djekhy (P. Louvre E 7834). We also met him
above in P. Louvre E 7833 and 7837 from 535 BCE. In P. Louvre E 7836
he once again leased a plot of land from Iturech, but we do not know
whether this was the same plot as before. The lease contract was written
by the overseer of the necropolis Neshor—short for Neshorpakhrat—
son of Petehorresne, another member of the famous family of scribes
(see above, "The Saite Restoration"). Neshor's brother Dykhonsuiut,
who is only known from this document, signed the contract as a witness, together with an equally obscure Mr. Nespasefy son of Pawakhhor.
Perhaps Dykhonsuiut was visiting the office of his brother on this day;
perhaps he worked there:

> Regnal year 35, third month of the shemu season under Pharaoh
> l.p.h. Amasis l.p.h. The cattle keeper of Montu Petemontu son of
> Pawakhamun has said to the choachyte Iturech son of Djekhy: "You
> have leased to me your mortuary foundation land that was given to
> you for the maintenance of the priest of Amun-Ra King of Gods
> Inaros son of Teskhonsu, located in the high land The Stable of the
> Milk Can of Amun, called The Sluice (?), its west being The Lamp

Land of Khonsu. When harvest has occurred in regnal year 36, we will divide all grain and all shoots that have come up into two shares. Specification: you will receive a share and I and my business partners will receive the other share. We will pay the harvest tax of the Domain of Amun together, us two. Profit and loss will be shared by us, us two." In the writing of Neshor son of Petehorresne, the overseer of the necropolis.

What makes P. Louvre E 7836 so special—apart from the fact that it was a written rather than an oral land lease—is the division of the harvest. The landlord Iturech of Djekhy & Son receives a full half of the harvest (before tax), whereas in a standard ancient Egyptian land lease this would be a quarter to a third. This land lease is clearly an exception, even if we do not know why. Because Petemontu and Iturech would share the 10 percent harvest tax equally, each would be left with 45 percent. Petemontu would then have to divide this among his business associates. We do not know who provided the seedcorn, but it is probably safe to say that Petemontu took care of the oxen needed to plow the land. He was, after all, a cattle keeper of the Domain of Montu.

The Lamp Land of Khonsu

The fields in the archive of Djekhy & Son often have rather prosaic names like The Stable of the Milk Can of Amun and The Land of the Servant of the Place of Truth. The Lamp Land of Khonsu was another. Khonsu was the divine child in the holy Theban triad of Amun, Mut, and Khonsu. Occasionally he did play a role in the lives of the Theban choachytes, for instance if someone had to take an oath to settle a (business) conflict. This was most likely done in the temple of Khonsuemwasneferhotep inside the walls of the immense temple compound of Amun.

The proceeds of a lamp land were used to buy wicks and oil to keep the lamps burning in the divine shrine. Fields like these were donated by the royal family and private individuals. Stela BM EA 952, from regnal year 1 of Pharaoh Amasis, was found in Kom al-Ahmar (al-Sawaris), about twenty kilometers south of al-Hiba on the east bank of the Nile. It concerns the donation of such a lamp land:

Regnal year 1, second month of the akhet season, day 1 under the majesty of (full titulary) [Amasis son of Neith], may he live forever, beloved by Horus of Hutnesu. On this day the donation (took place) of a field of ten aruras of dry land in the district of Shekek, to keep a lamp (burning) for Horus Lord of Hutnesu, under the authority of the doorkeeper of Horus Lord of Hutnesu Djeddjehutyiufankh son of Petiese.

Together with P. BM EA 10113, which was once temporarily kept in the archive of Djekhy & Son, this stela bears silent witness to the events that unfolded in rural Egypt in 570 BCE. It has been dated to 13 January 570 BCE, so technically this was still regnal year 20 of Pharaoh Apries, the predecessor of Amasis. But whereas the Theban scribe who wrote P. BM EA 10113 stubbornly clung to Apries as the ruling pharaoh as late as 19 October 570 BCE, the man who made stela BM EA 952 had reconciled himself to the new situation. This may be further evidence that it took some time for Amasis's power to extend as far south as Thebes, where P. BM EA 10113 was written.

Not a Real Land Lease

October 534 BCE (Papyrus Louvre E 7839)

How the beekeeper of Montu Peteatum and Iturech of Djekhy & Son became acquainted we do not know, but it may have been through Peteatum's business partner Petemontu, who was a cattle keeper of the same Domain of Montu. Somewhere in or before the year 534 BCE Peteatum had evidently become indebted to Iturech. The day on which this contract (P. Louvre E 7839) was written was beautiful. The weather was good, warm and sunny. Elsewhere in the world great events were taking place. At the age of twenty-nine a prince called Siddhartha—later to become the Buddha—decided to leave his father's castle and venture out into the world to find the truth.[1] On the other side of the planet the last true Roman king, Tarquinius Superbus, came to power. The best way to celebrate this occasion, in his view, was to have a large number of senators put to death and to revoke some of the concessions his predecessors had made to the plebeians. In Thebes, it was business as usual for Djekhy & Son.

One day in October 534 BCE Iturech and the beekeeper Peteatum were standing before the scribe Neshor son of Petehorresne, the overseer of the necropolis. Two years earlier the same Neshor had drawn up a land lease between Iturech and the cattle keeper Petemontu. What makes P. Louvre E 7839 interesting is that although it has all the characteristics of a land lease, it seems not to be one at all: after the harvest had occurred in

533 BCE, Peteatum would pay the harvest tax to the Domain of Amun and give the remainder to Iturech. In other words, Peteatum would get nothing for his trouble, which suggests that this agreement actually concerns the repayment of a debt. Also remarkable is that the land leased out by Iturech in P. Louvre E 7839 had been given to him to pay for the mortuary cult of the priest of Amun Djekhy son of Besmut.

By pure coincidence the coffin of Djekhy son of Besmut has survived. It is kept in the Cairo Museum under the inventory number CG 41011, but unfortunately no photograph has ever been published due to the state in which it was found. The official publication from 1912 by the French Egyptologist Alexandre Moret, *Sarcophages de l'époque Bubastite à l'époque Saïte* in the *Catalogue Général des antiquités égyptiennes du Musée du Caire* series described the actual state of the coffin as mediocre, which was enough to relegate the remains to a storehouse of the museum. However, with some imagination we can still see Iturech pouring his water offering next to it.

The link between this coffin and the archive of Djekhy & Son was made by the German demotist Günter Vittmann, and finds related to the Besmut family continue to be made to this day. As recently as 2006 about 1,150 fragments of Djekhy's Book of the Dead—which he took with him into his tomb—were found stored in Cairo. Part of this book has been reconstructed by the German Egyptologist Irmtraud Munro; she calculated that it must have been at least ten meters in length. It also mentions this other Djekhy's mother, a woman by the name of Tairy.

The Besmut Family

The Besmut family—named after at least ten members of this family called Besmut—was very influential in Thebes and can be traced back well into the Bubastite Period. This started c. 950 BCE and was named after Bubastis, the Delta hometown of Sheshonq I, the first Libyan ruler of the Twenty-second Dynasty. The name Besmut is rather rare outside this family, although it does occur. Most male members of the family had some position at the Theban temples, the temples of Montu and Amun being the favorites.

The family has been subjected to very thorough research by some of the brightest minds in Egyptology, resulting in a large number of extremely intricate family trees that have one thing in common: much like the family trees of humanity's earliest ancestors, they are likely to change the moment a new find is made. What we know so far is this: At one point the Besmut family married into the family of Montuem-hat, the famous mayor of Thebes under Pharaoh Taharqa, whose tomb in the Assasif counted no fewer than fifty-seven chambers. Members of the Besmut family are known from a large number of objects, from small statues to the famous Saite Oracle Papyrus from regnal year 14 of Psamtik I. Even as recently as 2004 a reference to a Hor son of Besmut, previously unknown but believed to be from the same family, surfaced in two abnormal hieratic papyri that probably date from the seventh century BCE. Named after the well-known antiquities dealer George Michaélides from Cairo, these papyri are now in the British Museum under the inventory numbers P. BM EA 10906 and 10907. Many coffins of priests of Montu belonging to the Besmut family were found together in a *cachette* in Deir al-Bahari in the Assasif, and perhaps this *cachette* or a nearby chapel was once the actual spot where the choachyte Iturech came to bring his funerary offerings. If the mummy of Djekhy son of Besmut—a known name sequence in this family—really did belong to the Besmut family, which is likely, this means Iturech provided his funerary services to people belonging to the highest circles in Thebes.

P. Louvre E 7839 is the last papyrus in the archive to mention Iturech, and the penultimate document in the archive:

Regnal year 37, second month of the shemu season under Pharaoh l.p.h. Amasis l.p.h. The beekeeper of the Domain of Montu Lord of Hermonthis, Peteatum son of Peteneferhotep, whose mother is Tary, has said to the choachyte of the valley Iturech son of Djekhy: "You have leased to me the field of the mortuary foundation that has been given to you for the maintenance of the tomb of the priest of Amun Djekhy son of Besmut. The south is the place (i.e., tomb) of Nesamun, the north is the place of Amunmetusneb, the west is the place of Efau, and the east is the dike of The Canals of the Scorpion (?). (This is) to cultivate it from regnal year 37 to regnal year 38. When harvest has occurred in regnal year 38 I will pay the harvest tax of the Domain of Amun for your field and I will give you the remainder of the harvest apart from the harvest tax that will come up on your field. I will leave your field, being far from it, starting from regnal year 38, second month of the shemu season, without citing any document." In the writing of Neshor son of Petehorresne, the overseer of the necropolis.

P. Louvre E 7839 offers little new information. It does, however, show once again how difficult the translation and interpretation of early demotic texts can be. When Peteatum refers to the payment of the harvest tax of the Domain of Amun and the delivery of the remainder to Iturech, the text literally says:

> When shemu has occurred in regnal year 38, I will pay the shemu of the Domain of Amun for your field and I will give you the remainder of the shemu apart from the shemu that will come up on your field.

The correct rendering of this passage did cause earlier authors—Michel Malinine and George Hughes—some trouble. The first two instances of 'shemu' present few difficulties because they also occur elsewhere in the same fixed order. The third instance, however, could be translated as either 'harvest' or 'harvest tax.' The same applies to the fourth instance of the term. Malinine tried to find a way out of this by translating the third instance as 'lease sum,' but this translation would be unique to this period. The translation in this book follows Hughes because it has the obvious advantage of being strictly logical.

To add to the confusion, it seems even the ancient Egyptian scribe found this clause a little awkward: what has been translated as 'apart from' is actually a preposition that is never used in this manner in other texts. Still, the gist of this clause seems clear: Peteatum will work the land, but will receive nothing in return. He will also have to deliver the harvest tax to the Domain of Amun. The tax receipt for this delivery is missing. And so—quietly—the business activities of the second owner of Djekhy & Son come to an end.

10

Water

Iturech 536 BCE

New Mummies, New Opportunities

November–December 536 BCE (Papyrus Louvre E 7843)

The year 536 BCE had been a rather hectic business year for Iturech, or at least one that was very well documented in P. Louvre E 7834, 7836, 7838, and 7843. Choachytes needed to collect as many mummies as possible. Many mummies meant much work, and much work meant high income. In 536 Iturech had an interest in at least five tombs in the Theban necropolis on the west bank of the Nile (Table 8).

The location of these tombs is unknown, even though tomb [5] may have been the *cachette* at the mortuary temple of Queen Hatshepsut in Deir al-Bahari. There is still a wide gap between the written early demotic material and the archaeological evidence. Some of the other tombs were without doubt located in the Assasif, where the most important tombs from the Late Period have been found. P. Louvre E 7843 from the winter of 536 BCE was all about the partial ownership of tombs [3] and [4]. Somewhere between 30 November and 30 December Iturech and the choachyte Khausenmut had a contract written by an otherwise unknown scribe. In this case we may assume that his colleague Khausenmut was also a friend. The business relation between their families went back to at least 559 BCE, twenty-three years earlier (P. Louvre E 7848). The families were so close that Iturech even kept the marital property agreement made out for Khausenmut's sister Tsendjehuty with his own papers (P. Louvre E 7846).

The contract made between Iturech and Khausenmut was not signed by witnesses. Perhaps it is a copy, and the original witnessed document was kept in Khausenmut's archive; perhaps neither man felt the need to have the contract witnessed. It is a straightforward contract:

Regnal year 35, fourth month of the shemu season under Pharaoh l.p.h. Amasis l.p.h. The choachyte of the valley Khausenmut son of Teos, whose mother is Ruru, has said to the choachyte of the valley Iturech son of Djekhy: "You are my sharing-partner in the place (i.e., tomb) of the mountain that we have given to the priest Petemestu son of Nespamety, and also in the place of the priest Djedmontui-ufankh son of Pakhar, regarding anything that will be given to us in their name, viz., bread, offerings, and all else that will be given in their name, half being yours and half being mine, and we will share their services between us, the two men, half being yours and half being mine, to complete (the specification)." In the writing of Inaros son of Petosiris.

A very clear contract indeed: There are two mummies, the choachytes provided a tomb for one of them, the families are prepared to pay for their mortuary cult, and Khausenmut appoints Iturech as his partner for half the income. It is obvious why Khausenmut and Iturech concluded this agreement. But it is nowhere stated what Iturech had to pay

Table 8. Iturech's tombs in the Theban necropolis

Tomb	Description
[1]	The rock tomb of the 'Great Ones': the rights to part of this tomb were already owned by Iturech's father Djekhy in 559 BCE, forming a partnership with the children of the choachyte Teos (P. Louvre E 7848)
[2]	The tomb of the priest of Amun-Ra King of Gods Inaros son of Teskhonsu (P. Louvre E 7836)
[3]	The rock tomb of the priest Petemestu son of Nespamety, in a partnership with the choachyte Khausenmut son of Teos, who was probably Djekhy's former business partner in tomb [1] above (P. Louvre E 7843)
[4]	The tomb of the priest Djedmontuiufankh son of Pakhar, in a partnership with the choachyte Khausenmut son of Teos, who was probably Djekhy's former business partner in tomb [1] above (P. Louvre E 7843)
[5]	The tomb of the priest of Amun Djekhy son of Besmut, whose coffin is now in the Cairo Museum (P. Louvre E 7839). We cannot exclude the possibility that tomb [5] was in reality tomb [1].

to acquire the partial rights to the mummies from tombs [3] and [4], even though this deal provided him with an income in the longer term by adding two more assets to his funerary business.

11

Cattle
Djekhy 533 BCE

Just a Priest from Thebes

29 November–29 December 533 BCE (Papyrus Louvre E 7850)

In the winter of 533 BCE, the overseer of the necropolis Peteamun son of Teos—another member of the famous Theban family of scribes described above in "The Saite Restoration" (he is the son of Teos son of Petehorresne)—dictated an official letter to his superior, a god's father of Amun called Djekhy. We know that this is not the same Djekhy as the first known owner of the archive of Djekhy & Son, because he vanishes somewhere around 550 BCE. However, the fact that P. Louvre E 7850 is the last document deposited in this archive, about eight years before the Persian invasion, at least suggests that this god's father of Amun may have been a son of the choachyte Iturech, although we cannot be certain. The context—an overseer of the necropolis, the payment of a mummy tax, and The God's Offering of Amun—seamlessly connects P. Louvre E 7850 with the rest of the archive and makes it reasonable for it to have been stored there. So what did the sender Peteamun have to say?

> May Ra grant that his (Djekhy's) life be long! The first prophet of Horweris Pamety son of Petehorpabik has handed to me this red bull that has been allotted to The God's Offering of Amun in the name of the fourth prophet of Horweris Petehorpabik, his father, to replace the commodities that are normally given to the overseer of the necropolis in the west of Thebes. I have received the bull described above and I have taken it out (to the pasture). My heart is satisfied with it. I am far from him in whatever issue in the name of the fourth prophet in the name of his burial in the west of Thebes.

This is an official letter to report that an otherwise unknown priest of the god Horweris has delivered a bull to pay for the burial or the transport of his father's mummy. The content of the letter is partly derived from the official legal formulae usually found in tax receipts. It was signed at the end by a scribe called Dykhonsuiut son of Qenhor. The bull was transferred to the overseer of the necropolis Peteamun himself, but apparently allotted to The God's Offering of Amun, the economic department of the temple of Amun.

The mummy mentioned in this letter may be what actually links it to the archive of Djekhy & Son. Maybe Iturech had been instrumental in the funeral in some way or other. The payment of the necropolis tax, however, was made by the son of the deceased in person.

Unless new related documents come to light, the reason P. Louvre E 7850 was deposited in the archive will remain a mystery. Many other questions also remain unanswered. If the god's father Djekhy, the addressee, was indeed the son of Iturech, what happened to his father? Why does the archive of Djekhy & Son end with this letter in 533 BCE? Is there any connection with the Persian invasion of 525 BCE? In 526 BCE the forty-four year reign of Amasis had ended. He was succeeded by his son Psamtik III, who lost the empire the next year. If, however, Djekhy was indeed the next in line to lead Djekhy & Son, it is obvious that he sought his fortune elsewhere, relegating his father's and grandfather's archive to the attic. In the end, we will probably never know.

12

Ink

Hieratic and Demotic: Why Bother?

This is actually the wrong question. Readers who have made it this far should by now have at least some idea of the importance of hieratic and demotic to our knowledge of ancient Egypt. The real question is: what else can we learn from it?

To answer this we will return to the village of Deir al-Medina. This site has produced many thousands of ostraca telling us all about everyday life in New Kingdom Egypt, at least for this village. The village itself was first excavated between 1905 and 1909 by the Italians under Ernesto Schiaparelli. Many of the ostraca they found were published in four volumes between 1978 and 1984 by the Egyptologist Jesús López in the *Catalogo del Museo Egizio di Torino: Ostraca Ieratici N. 57001–57568*. Although the Turin collection published by Jesús López contains a relatively large number of less important sources, these are still very useful for our purpose.

Between 1922 and 1951 Deir al-Medina was excavated again by the French under Bernard Bruyère. The French found two important sites near Deir al-Medina: the Grand Puits and the Kom du Sud. They were fortunate enough to have obtained the services of the talented Czech Egyptologist Jaroslav Černý. Černý published many hundreds of hieratic documentary ostraca in a manner that is unsurpassed to this day. In 1935 alone he published the first part of his *Catalogue des ostraca hiératiques non littéraires de Deir el Médineh* with 113 ostraca, along with a volume of the *Catalogue Général* for the Cairo Museum, *Ostraca hiératiques. Nos. 25501–25832*, to be followed by five more volumes in the series *Catalogue des ostraca hiératiques non littéraires de Deir el Médineh* of the IFAO—the Institut français d'archéologie orientale—in Egypt.

The IFAO ostraca series is now being continued to the same high standard by the French Egyptologist Pierre Grandet. At the end of the 1990s the *Deir al-Medina Database* was made available on the Internet by Egyptologists from Leiden University. It contains all the relevant data from approximately four thousand documentary ostraca (and papyri) that are kept in the most important collections. This scientific—and free—database aims to make the hieratic sources from Deir al-Medina accessible to a larger audience than just Egyptologists and to allow a quick assessment of the content of these sources.

Let us, however, start at the beginning. To publish a hieratic papyrus or ostracon we need access to the original source. Relying on a photograph is not good enough; mistakes can creep in too easily, as we saw with P. Louvre E 7855, where a hole in the papyrus was mistaken for ink because the photograph was taken against a dark background.

Egyptologists copy original papyri by tracing the ink markings onto plastic drawing film, the kind that was used to make cartoons in the days before computer animation. For a drawing pen, I have always depended on the Rotring 0.25 Rapidograph. Some Egyptologists put the drawing film directly onto the source itself, but this can be tricky. Most ostraca, whether pottery or limestone, tend to have an irregular surface, while papyri are always covered in (plexi)glass, which slightly distorts the focus. It is also possible to place the drawing film over a photograph of the ostracon or papyrus and trace the photograph, making sure constantly to compare what you are tracing against what you see on the original. Despite its apparent rigor, even this procedure will result in slight deviations from the original text. A magnifying glass is used for final checks and going over uncertain passages. The result of this painstaking work is called a facsimile (see for instance figure 4: P. Louvre E 7861).

One of the main advantages of a facsimile is that it is less distracting than a photograph because it is black on white. A facsimile may also show traces that are not visible on a photograph or, conversely, eliminate marks that look like ink but are not. There may be considerable differences between a photograph of a papyrus and what is actually there, as figure 8 reveals.

Drawing a facsimile is exhausting for the eyes. Some people are very good at it, others very bad. Part of the difficulty is that to make a good facsimile, it is necessary actually to know what the source says. A telling example is the name 'Wedjahorek' from the famous *Demotisches Namen-buch* (1980–2000), a lexicon listing names from countless demotic papyri. It is no coincidence of course that this Wedjahorek happens to be one of the minor characters from the archive of Djekhy & Son. But in P. Louvre E 7833, where he occurs as a landlord, he is called Wedjahor, not Wedjahorek. The mistake can be traced back to Michel Malinine. There is an auxiliary stroke of ink on the back of the papyrus, directly opposite the beginning of the official declaration *djed NN*, 'NN has said' on the front, which marks the place where the witnesses should sign to show that they had been present to hear Wedjahor's oral statement. Malinine misread this stroke as the grammatical element *k*, 'you, your,' which he appended to the name Wedjahor. In fact, the grammatical element *k* in demotic does look just like the little auxiliary stroke heading the list of witnesses. Although the editors of the *Demotisches Namenbuch* noted that this Wedjahorek named on the back of the papyrus must be the same man named as Wedjahor on the front, this ghost name—a good example of German thoroughness—still appears in the final publication as Wedjahorek. Rumor has it that the demotist who was given the job of making the facsimiles for the *Demotisches Namenbuch* in the Louvre had arrived in Paris with a generous grant, but most of it went up in smoke while he enjoyed Parisian nightlife. Only after some weeks did he finally set to work on the facsimiles, nursing a blinding hangover and thus not paying sufficient attention to catch the mistake.

In Černý's days a thorough publication of a hieratic ostracon (or papyrus) already consisted of a description—dimensions of the object, quality of the material, provenance, and so on, sometimes a photograph, a facsimile, a transcription into hieroglyphs, a translation (not always), and scientific notes (not always). In text publications the notes consist of palaeographical notes about special features of the script, difficult signs and passages, words left unread, and so on, along with notes about the content to give the textual source its place within the whole of our knowledge. If the textual source is a single short ostracon or easy to understand, there really isn't that much to say, so that we can dispense with the notes, as in Černý's publication of the Cairo ostraca: O. Cairo CG (*Catalogue Général*) 25752, which has a short description, a facsimile of the recto and verso, and a transcription of both sides into hieroglyphs. It is a short note from the Nineteenth or Twentieth Dynasty measuring 13 x 18 cm. Apart from a minor reading problem at the end of the first line on the back it says: "Don't say: 'I will sing,' because I will make sure you will not sing at all. Pasen is the one who will sing before Meresger!"

Meresger—'She loves silence'—was a highly popular cobra goddess in Deir al-Medina. She could help in case of illness and death, but also in love matters. But what is so striking about this short note is that the writer needed two sides of an ostracon the size of an A5 sheet (148 x 210 mm) for a very short message. This begins to make sense when we look at the size of the signs he used. The actual width of the first line shown below is 10 cm.

Figure 9. O. Cairo CG 25752 verso? [Courtesy Supreme Council of Antiquities Egypt; author's facsimile]

The last sign, the determinative—the hieroglyph at the end of a word marking the category to which it belongs, tree or fish for instance, here used by the scribe to mark not only the end of the name of the goddess Meresger (a cobra determinative) but also his message (it is at the bottom left)—almost looks like a 5-cm exclamation mark. It is a bold oblique stroke drawn all the way to the edge of the ostracon, as if the scribe is using it to express his own anger or frustration. Is it possible to reconstruct to some extent the mood of an ancient Egyptian scribe as he wrote an ostracon or papyrus? Could it really be that the rather fiercely written hieratic of O. Cairo CG 25752 actually reflects the scribe's anger? Other examples in this chapter seem to suggest that this may be so. In the case of who was to sing before Meresger, however, what Černý took to be the verso might in fact have been the front of the ostracon, which would then have read: "Pasen is the one who will sing before Meresger! Don't say: 'I will sing,' because I will make sure you will not sing at all." In that case our scribe would have written this 'exclamation mark' to end the first side of the note, just before he turned the ostracon to write the second line, still reflecting the anger he felt when writing this note.

Černý must have been aware that he was one of the very few Egyptologists of that time who could read hieratic well. It may be for precisely this reason that he published so many hieratic ostraca as photograph, facsimiles, and transcriptions, allowing others to benefit from his vast knowledge. The translation and interpretation of these ostraca would be reserved for a later date. Černý's own words show he was well aware that his work was only the beginning: "Whether and how far it will be possible to classify the variety of hands appearing in the documents of The Tomb (i.e., Deir al-Medina), and to link the handwritings with individual scribes, are questions which must also be left to future research." And he was uniquely placed to know that when working with ostraca from a specific period, for instance the reign of a particular pharaoh, an Egyptologist can develop an uncanny ability to single out individual styles. It is not a coincidence that Černý published specific ostraca—for example, O. Deir al-Medina 32–47—together (see further below). It is precisely this ability to distinguish between individual styles that promises to open up a whole new perspective on the approach to hieratic.

Let us for a brief moment return to the Turin ostraca published by Jesús López, O. Turin N. 57001–57568, scores of which are dated to the rule of Ramesses III (reigned 1194–1163 BCE). Jesús López noted that some of these ostraca looked very similar, for instance O. Turin N. 57028 and 57056; O. Turin N. 57031, 57032, and 57043; and O. Turin N. 57033 and 57038. Some of these are shown below.

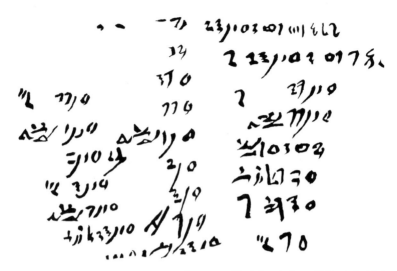

Figure 10. O. Turin N. 57033 recto [Courtesy Cisalpino Istituto Editoriale Universitario; author's facsimile]

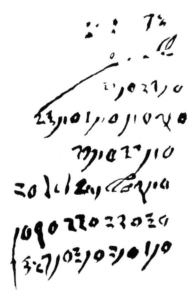

Figure 11. O. Turin N. 57038 verso [Courtesy Cisalpino Istituto Editoriale Universitario; author's facimile]

To understand the subject matter of these and many other ostraca from this Turin scribe, we will first translate the content of P. Turin N. 57033 recto. It is a working log of twenty-six lines in three separate columns. Two of these lines are now mere traces in the top left corner of the ostracon. Of col. II *l.* 9 and III *l.* 9 only the upper half remains. Since hieratic runs from right to left, the first column starts in the upper right corner of the ostracon. Some of the entries look very logical even today: 'day' is a small sun sign at the beginning of most lines; 'arrived' is expressed by legs walking, for instance at the end of col. I *l.* 4. In translation O. Turin N. 57033 becomes:

Regnal year 24, first month of the shemu season, day 25.
Regnal year 25, first month of the shemu season, day 26: (lamps) 5.
Day 27: (lamps) 5.
Day 28: no working. Arrived.
Second month of the shemu season, day 1: no working.
Day 2: in this place (Valley of the Queens).
Day 3: lamps 5.
Day 4: (lamps) 6.
(Column 2) Second month of the sh[emu season . . .].
Second month of the sh[emu season . . .].
Day 7.
Day 8.
Day 11: no working. Arrived.
Day 12.
Day 13.
Day 14: . . . (?).
Day 15: no working. Arrived.
(Column 3) [Day 16: . . .].
[Day 17: . . .].
Day 18: (lamps) 6.
Day 21: no working. Arrived.
Qenbet (local court of law). Day 22.
Day 23: (lamps) 6.
Day 24: no working. Arrived.
Day 25: in this place (Valley of the Queens).
Day 26: [. . .].

Not a very busy working week. Recall that the Egyptian week consisted of ten days. Note that the roster skips days 19–20 of the first month of shemu, as well as days 9–10 and 19–20 of the second month of shemu. These were the weekends.

To return to the cluster of Turin ostraca shown above, however, remarkably Jesús López did not take the next step. Had he done so, he would have noticed that the seven ostraca he selected—mostly dated to regnal years 24 and 25 of Ramesses III—had in fact all been written by a single scribe. Extensive research has shown that the same scribe also wrote O. Turin N. 57026, 57029, 57030, 57034, 57039, 57044, 57046, 57047, and 57055.

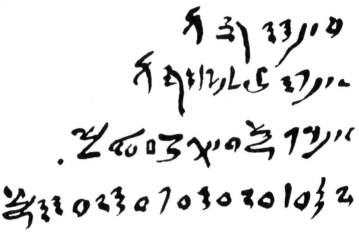

Figure 12. O. Turin N. 57047 recto *ll.* 4–7 [Courtesy Cisalpino Istituto Editoriale Universitario; author's facsimile]

O. Turin N. 57047 is another lamp account written by our scribe. In O. Turin N. 57033 (figure 10), the lamps used by the crew are denoted either by the lamp determinative as a substitute for the whole word followed by the number of lamps used or simply by stating the number used. Here in O. Turin N. 57047 recto *l.* 4 he uses this determinative ("Day 26: lamps 20"), whereas in *l.* 5 he writes the word in full: "Day 27: *khebes* lamps 20." Line 7 once again shows that the workload of the men from Deir al-Medina was not particularly heavy. After the weekend on days 29 and 30, which this scribe always skips in his notes, it says: "Second month of the akhet season day 1. Day 2. Day 3. Day 4. Day 5. Day 6: no working."

It should be noted, however, that what has been summarized above in a few pages is, in fact, the result of months of painstaking research involving hundreds of separate facsimiles. It all starts with a gut feeling, but then you actually have to find the proof to support it. Also, the fact that various ostraca were written by the same scribe is not a breathtaking observation in itself. The great advantage of working with clusters of ostraca instead of individual pieces is that clusters are much more informative. Once we start looking at clusters, a whole new world opens up.

Many factors influence how a scribe writes: whether writing material is smooth or uneven (like a limestone ostracon with a rough spot in the middle that will absorb the ink), or whether the addressee has a high enough status that you care about the quality of the handwriting. Other factors are also influential, such as a quarrel with your wife, a superior barring your promotion, or last night's visit to the bar around the corner. All these factors and many more should be evident—or rather could perhaps be made evident—in the handwriting.

Černý published O. Cairo CG 25782 as part of a series (25779–25785), which suggests that he knew these ostraca were all written by the same scribe. Most of them were found by Howard Carter to the east of tomb 47 in the Valley of the Kings, where they had been left in a rolled-up mat. The ostraca were written in the Nineteenth Dynasty. The scribe's handwriting is rather square and typical, which is partly also due to his habit of dipping his reed deep into the ink before starting to write, so that after a few very bold sign-groups the writing begins to fade and thin. This habit produces a handwriting that looks rather irregular, blotchy, and clumsy for a professional scribe. But O. Cairo CG 25784 was undoubtedly written by the same scribe, and here we see how halfway through this text, the scribe—frustrated?—throws away his reed and takes out a new one. Immediately the handwriting changes. It becomes markedly neater. Note, for instance, the difference between "third month of the shemu season" at the beginnings of *ll.* 9 and 11. Might this have anything to do with the fact that the mood of the scribe suddenly improved as well? A fountain pen caught in bad paper would have been just as irritating three thousand years ago. If so, this effectively means we can actually—or at least partly and in specific cases—reconstruct the mood of the ancient Egyptian scribe.

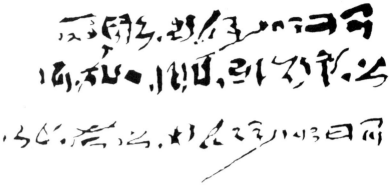

Figure 13. A new reed does wonders for the scribe's handwriting and probably also for his mood: O. Cairo CG 25784 *ll*. 9–11 [Courtesy Supreme Council of Antiquities Egypt; author's facsimile]

If we now look at one of the famous Late Ramesside Letters, we see that this may indeed apply to a number of texts written approximately three thousand years ago. LRL 15 (Papyrus Phillips) is a letter by the scribe Butehamun to his father, the scribe Djehutymose who was with the Egyptian army on a campaign in Nubia in the south. Butehamun was born and raised in or around Deir al-Medina. His father Djehutymose was a scribe of the necropolis, a high-ranking position. Butehamun would eventually—we have seen this happen often in the archive of Djekhy & Son—succeed to his father's position. But the village of Deir al-Medina was doomed. Ramesses XI (reigned 1100–1070 BCE) was the last pharaoh to have his tomb cut in the Valley of the Kings; from then on there was no more work. Most villagers had left by then, partly because the west bank of the Nile was becoming increasingly unsafe. Central authority had broken down, and according to some Egyptologists armed bands roamed the countryside, often Libyan mercenaries or nomads. Still, some of the old villagers would visit the village from time to time, because this was where their forefathers had been buried.

There is little doubt that Butehamun was one of them. We know he liked to walk in the immediate countryside because he left many graffiti in the Theban necropolis. He also kept the family archive—that of Djehutymose & Son—in his former parental home in Deir al-Medina. In a letter he reports an inspection of these personal papers after some heavy rains. Butehamun was an important man. He was to become one of the royal officials responsible for damage control in the Valley of the Kings. The fact that central authority was virtually nonexistent had allowed thieves to rob just about all the royal tombs. Butehamun was appointed to identify what remained of the royal mummies, rewrap them, and find a safe place for reburial.

This was to become tomb 35 in the Valley of the Kings, where the French Egyptologist Victor Loret in 1898 indeed found the mummies of, for instance, Amunhotep III, Merenptah, Sety II, and Ramesses IV, V, and VI. One other famous cache was found in Deir al-Bahari (DB 320), which was probably discovered as early as 1860 by Egyptian tomb robbers. They made the mistake of flooding the market with high-quality antiquities, thereby alerting the director of the Service d'Antiquités Égyptiennes to their find. This second cache contained the mummies of, among others, Seqenenra Tao II, Amunhotep I, Thutmosis II and III, Sety I, and Ramesses II and III. The linen wrapping of Ramesses III actually held a docket stating that the mummy had been restored by Butehamun:

Regnal year 13, second month of the shemu season, day 27 (?). On this day the high priest of Amun-Ra King of Gods Pinudjem gave the order to the scribe of the temple Djesersukhonsu and the scribe of the Place of Truth Butehamun to turn Pharaoh Usermara-Meryamun into Osiris, he being made firm (again) and enduring for eternity.

But we must return to P. Phillips (LRL 15), a letter by Butehamun to his father Djehutymose. The beginning of an ancient Egyptian letter is often rather tedious, invoking a myriad of deities to look after the well-being of the addressee (as was seen above in the letter to the vizier Ta, "A Five-thousand-year Tradition"). The context of the letter is often missing, prompting Alan Gardiner, one of the greatest Egyptologists of the twentieth century, to make the following acute observation when he published two letters from the Ramesside Period, P. Valençay 1 and 2:

Of all Egyptian secular writings letters are apt to be the dreariest and least satisfying. In the normal Ramesside letter a substantial portion is devoted to fulsome greetings couched in stereotyped phraseology, and the rest may consist of enquiries after the health of this woman or that child, expressions of anxiety lest the cattle should not have been properly fed, requests for grain or money—in short, domesticities such as occur the world over and shed no light on the peculiar characteristics of pharaonic civilisation.

In P. Phillips this flowery introduction is written in uncial hieratic, the sort of hieratic used for religious texts. These are the signs at the beginnings of *ll.* 2–3:

Figure 14. P. Phillips *ll.* 2–3 (beginnings) [Courtesy The British Museum; author's facsimile]

Soon, however, we see the scribe—still writing in the upper half of the papyrus—become aware that he is using up writing space too fast; he shifts to using smaller signs (in line 4). These are the beginnings of *ll.* 7–8:

Figure 15. P. Phillips *ll.* 7–8 (beginnings) [Courtesy The British Museum; author's facsimile]

About halfway through, in *l.* 9, the scribe suddenly switches to Ramesside administrative hieratic. This is where the actual letter starts with the standard introduction: "When my letter reaches you. . . ." Ramesside administrative hieratic looks much more scribbled and untidy.

Figure 16. P. Phillips *l.* 9 (middle) [Courtesy The British Museum; author's facsimile]

What happened here? Maybe Butehamun wrote the first part of the text—up to *l.* 8 or so—when he had time, one sunny afternoon. Maybe he finished the letter during office hours, when he was pressed for time. But if we look at the content of the letter, we see that it says things like: "Don't stand in the line of spears thrown down," or "Make sure you return in one piece." Butehamun even asks his father to write to him in his own handwriting so he knows his father is still alive. Might this help to explain the untidy lower half of P. Phillips? One wonders whether Butehamun wrote the whole introduction as a matter of routine and only really started to worry about the danger his father was in when he began the actual letter in *l.* 9, a shiver running down his spine.

One important influence on handwriting (as well as the content and layout of letters) is the profession of the sender—whether, for instance, he was a vizier or a minor official. In ancient Egypt, the phenomenon was only noticed when the Late Ramesside Letters were republished, this time with photographs. This new publication distinguished between 'letters' and 'communications.' The author noted that communications never had a flowery introduction like P. Phillips. Also, the address would be as brief as possible. According to this criterion, the letters sent by General Piankhy—accompanied during his campaign by the scribe Djehutymose, Butehamun's father—were not letters, but communications. Whenever I speak to my mother on the telephone we will spend half an hour discussing irrelevant details, up to and including the medical problems of the mayor. By the time I am able to get my message across I have usually forgotten what it was. Whenever I spoke to my late father on the telephone, these conversations suddenly became miracles of efficiency. My father was in the army, just like Piankhy. And Piankhy had better things to do than dictate long, flowery introductions. So the sender's profession is also something to keep in mind if we look at letters. As is the profession of the addressee, for that matter.

Let us return to O. Turin N. 57001–57568 published in Jesús López, *Catalogo del Museo Egizio di Torino*. The sixteen ostraca written by the same scribe in the reign of Ramesses III—O. Turin N. 57026, 57028–57034, 57038–57039, 57043–57044, 57046–57047, and 57055–57056—have been studied in detail during the past few years. New ostraca written by the same scribe have been found in Turin, Cairo, Oxford, and Strasbourg. So far about twenty-five ostraca written by him are known. What do they teach us? Simple little things—for instance, that O. Turin N. 57055 was finished on day 25 of the first month of the shemu season in regnal year 24 of Ramesses III. On that day the scribe started a new ostracon, O. Turin N. 57033 (figure 10), dating it to regnal year 24, first month of the shemu season, day 25. However, the second line reads: regnal year 25, first month of the shemu season, (day) 26. This was the day Ramesses III had come to the throne. We can infer from this that the scribe started a new set of records in the new administrative year, just as we do today. The same happened in the Turin Strike Papyrus (P. Turin 1880), which we have already looked at. This report was written by the famous scribe Amunnakhte. The last entry about the troubles in Deir al-Medina relating to arrears in payments was made on day 25 of the first month of shemu in regnal year 29 of Ramesses III. The next day his thirtieth regnal year began, so the records were closed.

Or take, for instance, O. Turin N. 57034 and O. Valley of Queens 6. The latter was found in the spring of 1986 near tomb 48, more than eighty years after O. Turin N. 57034 was discovered. We can, however, reasonably infer that at some time, our Turin scribe carried both these documents together in his bag. O. Turin N. 57034 covers the use of lamps for days 4–28 of the second month of shemu in regnal year 22; O. Valley of Queens 6 covers days 1–23 of the third month of shemu. Since the scribe skipped days 9–10 and 19–20 in O. Turin N. 57034, he probably also skipped days 29–30. In the translation of O. Turin N. 57033 above, it was seen that this scribe had the habit of doing this. So when the weekend that ended O. Turin N. 57034 was over (days 29–30), the ostracon remained in his bag and he then started on the first day of the new month on a pristine ostracon that was later to become O. Valley of Queens 6.

There was one colleague and contemporary of the Turin scribe—one of the many we know from the village—whose ostraca span the period between regnal year 25 of Ramesses III and the first years of Ramesses IV. Deir al-Medina was administered by a number of scribes. The working crew that cut out and decorated the tombs in the Valley of the Kings (and the Valley of the Queens) worked in two shifts: there was a right crew and a left crew, each with effectively its own administrators. There were all kinds of deliveries to the village: visitors from the Theban temples, official visits by the vizier, workmen who had fallen ill, people involved in legal proceedings, and so on. All this had to be recorded in writing. The authorities were very keen to know what happened in the village. The first volume of the series *Catalogue des ostraca hiératiques non littéraires de Deir el-Medineh* started by Jaroslav Černý contains sixteen ostraca written by this particular scribe: O. DeM (Deir al-Medina) 32–47. Strikingly, many of these ostraca cover exactly one administrative month.

Figure 17 shows our scribe on a good day. Note that he started his records on the convex side of a potsherd (making this the recto), meaning that he probably rested this shard of 25.5 x 16 cm on his knee when writing. This, together with the fact that this is a two-dimensional photograph of a three-dimensional object, probably also helps to explain the upward slant of the line. In line 6 of O. DeM 40, the scribe recorded some deliveries of firewood. Even without any knowledge of ancient Egyptian it is possible to make out the word for woodcutter in the middle of the line, consisting of a knife above the striking arm determinative indicating activity: "First month of the akhet seaon, day 8. (On watch) Iyerniutef. From woodcutter Amunhotep 145 pieces of firewood."

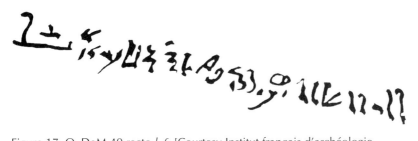

Figure 17. O. DeM 40 recto *l.* 6 [Courtesy Institut français d'archéologie orientale; author's facsimile]

In antiquity, this ostracon was larger than it is today. The entire top has broken off and is now kept in a French collection as O. Strasbourg H 42. If the two pieces were joined together, what is now *l.* 1 of the ostracon would then become *l.* 7, *l.* 6 in figure 17 would be *l.* 12. One does wonder whether the workmen in charge of the daily deliveries—their names are mentioned immediately after the day dates—were really expected to count the pieces of firewood that were delivered; the scribe certainly must have had to make sure the books were balanced. In any case, probably on day 9 the scribe reminded himself that some of the arrears were still due, so he wrote a marginal note conveniently staked off by a thick line to the left of *ll.* 6–7: "Remainder of the builder for the five extra days of regnal year 1. Remainder of firewood 690."

This was a highly professional scribe, but once he was forced to continue on the concave side of the ostracon his writing became decidedly sloppier.

Figure 18. O. DeM 44 verso *l.* 3 [Courtesy Institut français d'archéologie orientale; author's facsimile]

Apparently this scribe had a talent for selecting pottery sherds that could contain a thirty-day log. As for any good bookkeeper, the month was only officially finished if all the required deliveries had been made and recorded. More than once we see that on the last—thirtieth—day of the month the deliveries of firewood by the woodcutters fell short. Whenever this happened the scribe would copy the amounts due onto the ostracon covering the next month.

Černý's publication does not contain any photographs of O. DeM 32, 36, 37, 39 (+ 174), 43, or 47, but the layout and the datings mentioned in his transcriptions suggest that Černý himself was convinced, as we are, that these ostraca were all written by the same scribe. Černý did of course see the original sources. In all probability this scribe was Hori, a well-known character in Egyptology. The provenance also suggests that this is a closed group. As far as we can tell, most ostraca from this group were found between 18 and 20 January 1930 at one of the major French findspots, the Kom du Sud, suggesting that they were discarded together and had always been kept together in Hori's archive.

Let us now look at O. DeM 45. As in O. DeM 40, above, each day of the month is followed by the name of the workman on duty for that day, and all deliveries, however small, were meticulously recorded: fish, bread, beer, firewood, cakes, dates, figs, oil, and so on. Important events were also recorded, like the visit by the vizier to find a good spot for a new royal tomb in the Valley of the Kings. When we consider that we are looking over the shoulder of a bookkeeper who died about three thousand years ago, this depth of detail becomes rather thrilling. In *ll.* 15–17 Hori records a visit to the village by the vizier:

> Arriving that the overseer of the city and vizier Neferrenpet did in Thebes together with Pharaoh's butler Hori and Pharaoh's butler Amunkhau son of Tekhy. Day 18: they went to the valley [. . .] to select a spot for cutting out the tomb of Ramesses IV [. . .].

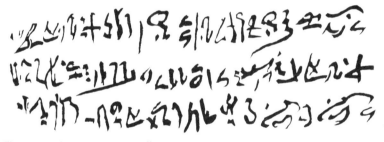

Figure 19. O. DeM 45 recto *ll.* 15–17 [Courtesy Institut français d'archéologie orientale; author's facsimile]

The records end with the conveniently planned distribution of salaries to the crew, obviously connected with the vizier's visit. He was on an important mission and could probably do with some peace and quiet in the village. This visit by the vizier may have been a once-in-a-lifetime event for a scribe from Deir al-Medina. In fact, this note about the vizier coming over to find a suitable spot for the tomb of Ramesses IV had a spectacular effect on Hori's mood and handwriting. If we compare this passage to Hori's entire corpus—O. DeM 32–47—we find that the signs are bigger, bolder, and wilder than ever before. The signs and sign-groups are almost dancing. Hori's sense of duty tells him that he should write this down—he is, after all, one of the village scribes—but his heart is racing while he does this. The exuberance of his handwriting effortlessly bridges the three-thousand-year gap between our emotions and his.

Once the premise is accepted that an Egyptian scribe's handwriting can be a clue to his mood, even after three millennia, we can turn again to the vast collection of Deir al-Medina. One very famous ostracon is O. BM EA 65930, also known as O. Nash 1. It is the official protocol of a legal case against a female thief in Deir al-Medina. It was written in regnal year 6 of (probably) Sety II (c. 1208 BCE). Mrs. Herya is accused of having stolen a copper chisel, which because of the metal was inherently valuable. Crimes like these were dealt with by a court of law called the *qenbet*, mostly consisting of the village dignitaries, often supplemented by religious or secular authorities. If such cases were tried in public, scores of people from the village may have been there to watch the events unfold. The accusation against Mrs. Herya came from the workman Nebnefer, and 'proof' was offered by a woman called Nebuemnehbet, who claimed to have witnessed the theft in a vision. Naturally Herya protested her innocence, but when an official from the court searched her house, he found not just the chisel, but also a metal object belonging to Amun of the Beautiful Encounter, a god invoked in the famous letter to the vizier Ta (see above, "A Five-thousand-year Tradition"). This was a very serious crime, and things looked bleak for Herya. The case was so serious that judgment was postponed until the arrival of the vizier. The ostracon closes with a list of the people who were members of the *qenbet* and an official note about an earlier, similar crime. But these do not concern us here. What we would like to know is how the scribe felt when he took these minutes.

O. Nash 1 was acquired by the British Museum in 1959 from Spinks & Son, after the first useful facsimile of the text had been published in Černý-Gardiner, *Hieratic Ostraca* (1957). The ostracon measures 26 x 18.5 cm. The text on the front consists of seventeen lines, some of which are damaged at the beginning. From *l.* 1 up to and including *l.* 11, the text is written in a very neat and precise hieratic. The signs and sign-groups in *ll.* 12–17 appear to be somewhat larger and bolder, which may be due to the scribe's reed wearing down. There is some extra spacing above and below *l.* 11, which was probably intentional. This line clearly marks some sort of turning point in this official protocol. In *l.* 10 Herya swears under oath that she is innocent. Tension mounts, in the court and with the scribe.

Although the first part of the protocol is flawless, suddenly above the line in *l.* 10—the moment of the oath—the scribe is obliged to make a correction. This oath, which begins with the formula "As Amun endures, as the Ruler l.p.h. endures," is the direct predecessor of the oath encountered in abnormal hieratic P. Louvre E 7861, written centuries later (see above, "Trustee"). This was the moment of truth for Herya. Nothing less than her life was at stake, and the scribe was probably so focused on what was happening that he wrote, "As Amun endures, as the endures" and had to insert 'Ruler l.p.h.' above the line afterward. Even stranger is the fact that he never finished recording Herya's oath: halfway through *l.* 11 he stops in mid-sentence: ". . . and one finds that I have stolen this chisel . . . ."

In *l.* 12 the protocol is resumed with a note explaining the interruption: an hour during which Mrs. Herya was questioned. This most probably included torture. It is not unlikely that the actual mistakes—admittedly not apparent to the untrained eye—made in *ll.* 13 and 14 by this highly professional scribe were somehow related to Herya's interrogation.

This phenomenon also applies to demotic. The scribe who copied the Ptolemaic demotic P. BM EA 10413—a contract dealing with an inheritance—in 124 BCE did so on a piece of papyrus that is now kept in the Rijksmuseum van Oudheden in Leiden as P. Leiden I 375. He obviously scanned the original before he started to write. Up to the beginning of the official contract starting with *djed NN,* 'NN has said,' the standard Ptolemaic demotic contract always lists the present and previous rulers as well as the most important priests attached to the royal cults. This is a rather long and boring dating formula, occupying the first five lines of P. BM EA 10413:

Regnal year 46, first month of the peret season, day 10 under Pharaoh l.p.h. Ptolemy VIII l.p.h. the beneficent god, son of Ptolemy V l.p.h. and Queen . . . Cleopatra III l.p.h., his wife, the beneficent gods, and the priest of Alexander and of the saving gods, the fraternal gods, the beneficent gods, the gods who love their father, the gods who appear, the god who loves his mother, the god who exalts his father, the beneficent gods, and the bearer of the trophy of victory before Berenice the Beneficent and the bearer of the golden basket before Arsinoe the Brother-loving, and the priestess of Arsinoe the Father-loving, in accordance with those who have been appointed in Alexandria and who have been appointed in Ptolemais in the Theban nome. NN has said (. . .).

One can almost imagine what the scribe of P. Leiden I 375 was thinking. It was an easy job of copying a contract. Judging by his handwriting he was not in the mood to deliver a neatly written copy today. He probably wondered whether this standard introduction was really necessary. Most readers were likely to skip the introductory formula anyway and start directly at the beginning of the contract, which was always clearly identifiable. To cut his work short, after stating in the first line of P. Leiden I 375 that this was a copy, he summarized the lengthy introduction of P. BM EA 10413 to save some time: "Regnal year 46, first month of the peret season, day 10 according to the titulary of Pharaoh l.p.h. (. . .)."

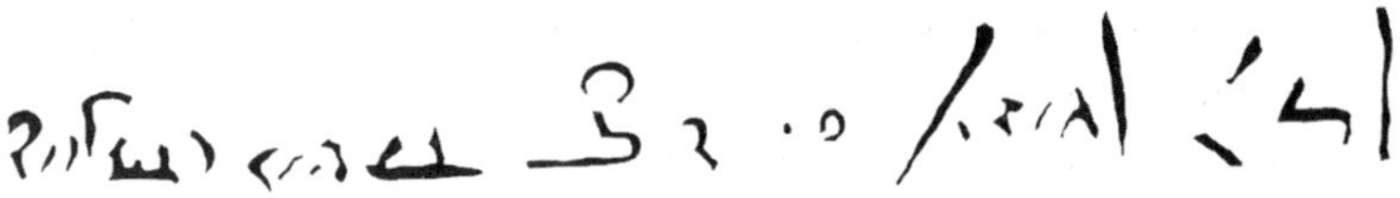

Figure 20. Unpublished P. Leiden I 375 *l.* 2 [Courtesy Rijksmuseum van Oudheden; author's facsimile]

Specific examples where the scribe runs into trouble of some kind are also seen in the archive of Djekhy & Son. Recall P. Louvre E 7847, for instance, where the scribe Petehorresne's inability to fit the final word of the contract at the end of the line caused him to make a writing mistake; he had possibly been irritated by the fact that his perfect layout was wrecked (see figure 6). If we look at P. Leiden E 7861 in figure 4, written by the same scribe, we see him lose interest after the very neatly written *l.* 1, although he is able to contain his urge to hurry for a few more lines. The last three lines before the horizontal break in the papyrus, however, show that by then his concentration had gone.

The scribe of the mat Petemestu wrote P. Louvre E 7834, 7835, 7838, and 7842, four tax receipts belonging to the archive of Djekhy & Son. Most of the mistakes he made—which occur more frequently than one would expect from a professional scribe—occur either at the beginning or at the end of a line; it seems Petemestu may have experienced a slight loss of focus moving from one line to the next.

We can also sympathize with the apprehension that must have been felt by the scribe who wrote P. Louvre E 7833. Before starting to write, a scribe would always assess how much space he would need, something that would automatically also decide his choice for the length of the first line, and in turn the length of all subsequent lines. The aim would be to achieve the optimal balance between the text and the amount of papyrus used. Scribes wanted their contracts to look good as well as being flawlessly written. When this scribe started to write P. Louvre E 7833, he made sure there was ample space between the lines. However, after a few lines he noticed that he was using up his writing space faster than he had anticipated—it was a rather complicated land lease—and so he was forced to use smaller signs, write more signs in each line, and reduce the spacing between the lines. With this correction, he still managed to squeeze his text into the available space, but only just.

A targeted survey of all the extant abnormal hieratic and demotic texts would produce many more examples, but that falls outside the scope of this book, which is about the people who kept the archive of Djekhy & Son. Almost 2,500 years passed before their papers became public. Many questions have been resolved and many remain. It is hoped, however, that this book has brought the Theban choachytes of the firm Djekhy & Son one step closer to their dream of immortality, which was also their main business.

Notes

Notes to Chapter 1

1 An Egyptologist studying the demotic script and the contemporary native Egyptian culture is called a demotist.

2 An introduction to P. Mattha is found at the end of this chapter.

3 For a beautiful artist's impression of what ancient Thebes and The House of the Cow may have looked like, see S. Aufrère, J.-C. Golvin, and J.-C. Goyon, *L'Égypte restituée* (1997).

Notes to Chapter 2

1 It is now being replaced, or rather supplemented, by the freely accessible web-based demotic dictionary published by the Oriental Institute in Chicago.

2 In both demotic and abnormal hieratic texts, the pious wish 'life, prosperity, health' was added, which is abbreviated as 'l.p.h.' by Egyptologists.

3 P. Cairo CG 30661 is another papyrus fragment kept in the Egyptian Museum that was probably written by one of these two men.

4 The facsimiles in this book were all prepared by the author on a PC without recourse to the original sources. They do not claim accuracy, but are intended only to clarify specific points.

5 Early demotic legal texts are dated to a specific month in regnal year X of a king. The abnormal hieratic texts often also mention the precise day.

Notes to Chapter 3

1 The Egyptian civil calendar had three seasons of four months each: akhet, peret, and shemu. The months comprised thirty days each, and there were five extra 'festival' days at the end of the year. There was no leap year, and

the 365-day civil calendar did not quite match the actual solar year, with the result that over time the solar year, the civil calendar, and the agricultural year fell out of sync (see below, "Egyptian New Year").

Notes to Chapter 4

1   It may be that Khausendjehuty was a half-brother of the children of the choachyte Teos, from another mother. If that is true, his mother's name (Takheru) would have been included to show where he stood in the family hierarchy. Since Teos is a very common Theban name, we cannot be certain of this interpretation.

2   The overseer of the necropolis also attended the celebration of the new year by the Theban choachytes; see below, "The Patron Saint."

3   In theory, the Petosiris mentioned in P. Louvre E 7840 could also be the grandson of the Petosiris mentioned in P. Louvre E 7848.

Notes to Chapter 5

1   This is the case in P. Louvre E 7845A, in which a single tenant rents more fields than the fifteen lessees from P. BM EA 10432 combined.

2   In 2003–2004 one average hectare in Egypt yielded approximately 8.54 tons, which is more than 16,000 liters.

3   Malinine in *Revue d'Égyptologie* 8 (1951): P. Louvre E 7833, 7844, and 7845A; Hughes, *Saite Demotic Land Leases* (1952): P. BM EA 10432, P. Louvre E 7833, 7836, 7837, 7839, 7844, and 7845A; Malinine, *Choix de textes juridiques en hiératique anormal et en démotique* (1953): P. Louvre E 7836, 7837, 7839, and 7843. After Malinine's death a transcription in hieroglyphs of P. Louvre E 7846 was published in *Revue d'Égyptologie* 34 (1982–83). In 1983 Malinine's former students published *Choix de textes juridiques en hiératique anormal et en démotique* II.

4   Note that this fraction also occurs in the tax receipt P. Louvre E 7841, quoted above in "Into the Flax Business."

5   The Benben stone was a holy stone kept in the temple of Heliopolis, symbolizing the primeval mound on which Atum created the world through masturbation.

Notes to Chapter 6

1   This letter was written on a reused papyrus (called a palimpsest) showing traces of what once was regnal year 20$^+$ (of Amasis), which allows us to conclude that it was written some time after 550 BCE.

2 The milk can mark is mentioned in P. Turin 2128 and P. Loeb 41, dating to 487 and 485 BCE.

3 These receipts were written by the same scribe and have until recently been mixed up in the literature; see above, "P. Louvre E 7834 and 7838."

Notes to Chapter 7

1 For a more detailed discussion, see above, "Working the Land."

Notes to Chapter 8

1 For this signature of Iturech, see figure 7. The possibility cannot be excluded that this was a namesake also called Iturech son of Djekhy, even if this would be some strange coincidence. However, as was seen above ("The Archive of Djekhy & Son"), namesakes did exist.

Notes to Chapter 9

1 Although recent scholarly opinion suggests the Buddha may actually have lived a century later.

Indexes

Deities
Rulers and officials
Private persons
Place names
Sources
General

MK = Middle Kingdom
NK = New Kingdom
O. = Ostracon
P. = Papyrus
St. = Stela

Deities

177

Takelot III 77
Thutmosis II 161
Thutmosis III 17, 161
Thutmosis IV 64
Tutankhamun 13, 79

Private persons
Ahauty (NK) 65
Amunhotep 1
Amunhotep (NK) 115, 165
Amuniu son of NN 42
Amunkhau son of Tekhy (NK royal
   butler) 167
Amunmetusneb 143
Amunnakhte (NK scribe) 63, 64, 164
Ankhhor son of Hor 119, 120, 121
Ankhhor son of Iturech 57, 70
Anyuuchay son of Iturech 8, 119, 120
Arenamun son of Heryesnef 23
Besmut 5, 109, 126, 137, 138, 142,
   143, 146
Butehamun son of Djehutymose (NK)
   160, 161, 163
Chayutayudeny son of Peteamunip
   27, 75, 76, 94, 95, 96, 97
Djedbastetiufankh son of Psamtik-
   menekh 111
Djeddjehutyiufankh son of Petiese
   141
Djedkhonsuiufankh 1
Djedkhonsuiufankh son of Rery 103,
   104, 105, 110, 111
Djedmontuiufankh son of Pakhar 146
Djedmutiufankh son of Inaros 131
Djefmin 44, 45, 46
Djehutyirtais son of Petehorpakhrat
   76
Djekhy (namesake) 17
Djekhy (priest) 9, 149
Djekhy & Son (business) see Index F
Djekhy son of Ankhkhratnefer 88
Djekhy son of Besmut 142, 143, 146
Djekhy son of Nadjedkara 44
Djekhy son of Tesmontu 1, 2, 3, 5, 8,
   16, 21, 22, 23, 24, 27, 32, 33, 35, 37,
   38, 39, 40, 41, 42, 43, 44, 45, 46, 50,
   51, 57, 58, 64, 67, 68, 69, 70, 71, 72,

73, 75, 76, 78, 83, 87, 88, 89, 90, 94,
   95, 96, 97, 98, 99, 101, 102, 106,
   118, 119, 120, 121, 135, 146, 149
Djesersukhonsu (NK) 161
Dyamunpankh 23
Dykhonsuiut son of Petehorresne 27,
   28, 139
Dykhonsuiut son of Qenhor 150
Efau 143
Efau (grandfather of Psamtik son of
   Ankhpakhrat) 94
Esekheb 95
Hemes (mother of Chayutayudeny)
   94
Hepy son of Teos 37, 38
Herya (NK) 168, 169
Hetepamun (mother of Pakhork-
   honsu) 23
Hetepamun son of Dyamunpankh 23
Hor son of Amunirankh 76
Hor son of Besmut 137, 143
Hor son of Iby 28
Hor 'son' of Iturech 8, 133, 134, 135,
   136, 137, 138
Hor son of Neshorbehedety 76
Hor son of Paybes 125
Hor son of Petiese 133
Hor son of Wesirweris 122
Hori (NK royal butler) 167
Hori (NK scribe) 63, 166, 167
Horkheb son of Khonsuirau 76
Horkhonsu son of Ituru 36
Horsiese son of Petebastet 90
Horwedja (grandfather of Horwedja
   son of Wennefer) 111
Horwedja son of Payfchauawybastet
   81, 82
Horwedja son of Wennefer (and grand-
   son of Horwedja) 21, 111, 112
Huy 1, 65
Ihudjehuty son of Inaros 76
Imouthes son of Wedjahor 137
Inaros son of Petehorresne 76
Inaros son of Petemin 58, 59
Inaros son of Petosiris 146
Inaros son of Teskhonsu 107, 139, 146
Ip son of Montirtais 23

Sources